The Metaphysics of Existence and Nonexistence

Also available from Bloomsbury:

God, Existence, and Fictional Objects, by John-Mark L. Miravalle
Knowledge and Reality in Nine Questions, by Matthew Davidson
Material Objects in Confucian and Aristotelian Metaphysics,
by James Dominic Rooney
The Metaphysics of Contingency, by Ferenc Huoranszki
Wittgenstein and the Problem of Metaphysics, by Michael Smith

The Metaphysics of Existence and Nonexistence

Actualism, Meinongianism, and Predication

Matthew Davidson

BLOOMSBURY ACADEMIC
LONDON • NEW YORK • OXFORD • NEW DELHI • SYDNEY

BLOOMSBURY ACADEMIC
Bloomsbury Publishing Plc
50 Bedford Square, London, WC1B 3DP, UK
1385 Broadway, New York, NY 10018, USA
29 Earlsfort Terrace, Dublin 2, Ireland

BLOOMSBURY, BLOOMSBURY ACADEMIC and the Diana logo are trademarks of
Bloomsbury Publishing Plc

First published in Great Britain 2023
This paperback edition published 2024

Copyright © Matthew Davidson, 2023

Matthew Davidson has asserted his right under the Copyright, Designs and
Patents Act, 1988, to be identified as Author of this work.

Cover image: Cagdas/Adobe Stock

All rights reserved. No part of this publication may be reproduced or transmitted
in any form or by any means, electronic or mechanical, including photocopying,
recording, or any information storage or retrieval system, without prior
permission in writing from the publishers.

Bloomsbury Publishing Plc does not have any control over, or responsibility for, any
third-party websites referred to or in this book. All internet addresses given in this
book were correct at the time of going to press. The author and publisher regret any
inconvenience caused if addresses have changed or sites have ceased to exist, but can
accept no responsibility for any such changes.

A catalogue record for this book is available from the British Library.

A catalog record for this book is available from the Library of Congress.

ISBN: HB: 978-1-3503-4483-9
PB: 978-1-3503-4487-7
ePDF: 978-1-3503-4484-6
eBook: 978-1-3503-4485-3

Typeset by Newgen KnowledgeWorks Pvt. Ltd., Chennai, India

To find out more about our authors and books visit www.bloomsbury.com
and sign up for our newsletters.

For Renee

Contents

Preface	ix
Introduction	1
1 Independence Actualism Explicated	3
2 The Independence Thesis	13
3 The Utility of Independence Actualism	41
4 Actualism or Meinongianism?	59
5 "Exists" as a Predicate	67
6 Existence and Essence	91
7 Robust and Deflationary Meinongianism	113
8 God and Necessary Existence	139
Notes	159
Bibliography	167
Index	179

Preface

In some ways this book was a long time coming. For nearly my entire philosophical career, I have been drawn to issues in the metaphysics of existence and nonexistence. I remember clearly where I was sitting in graduate school when I first read Nathan Salmon's "Existence" and the papers from John Pollock, Kit Fine, and Alvin Plantinga on the metaphysics of existence in the 1985 *Alvin Plantinga* volume. I found the material in all of those papers really exciting then (and I still do!). But the proximate cause of my writing this occurred a few years ago when I read Karel Lambert's excellent *Meinong and the Principle of Independence*. While reading it, it occurred to me that one may address a number of philosophical problems if objects that didn't exist could nevertheless exemplify properties and stand in relations. That realization caused me to write this book. I have many people to thank for helping me to bring this book to fruition. Thanks to two referees for Bloomsbury for very helpful comments on the manuscript. Thanks to John Mumma, Chris Menzel, John Nolt, Mike Byrd, Tom Crisp, Nino Cocchiarella, Gordon Barnes, Tony Roy, and Ed Wierenga for discussion of issues in the book. Special thanks to Jim Van Cleve and Tony Roy who provided extensive comments on the book manuscript. Thanks to my dean, Rueyling Chuang, for allowing me time away from teaching so that I could write this book. My editor at Bloomsbury, Colleen Coalter, was incredibly helpful in getting the manuscript ready for publication; as was Suzie Nash. It will be evident to the reader the debt I owe to Alvin Plantinga in the way I approach issues in the metaphysics of existence and nonexistence. I am grateful both for his philosophical work and for the time he invested in my own formation as a philosopher.

Introduction

This is a book about the metaphysics of existence and nonexistence. My primary aim is exploring a view that I call *independence actualism*: That (i) objects may exemplify properties and stand in relations at worlds and at times where they don't exist, and (ii) necessarily, there are no objects that don't exist. This isn't the only aim, however. We also will consider the issue of whether "exists" is a predicate, which sort of Meinongian one should be if one is to be a Meinongian, existentialism (in Plantinga's [1983] sense), and God's relation to necessarily existing abstracta. Thus, this is a wide-ranging book in the metaphysics of existence and nonexistence.

The book comprises eight chapters. In Chapter 1, I state independence actualism more thoroughly and consider different ways of formulating actualism *simpliciter*. There, I argue that independence actualism is really an actualist view. In Chapter 2, I defend the independence thesis: the proposition that objects may exemplify properties and stand in relations at worlds and at times where they don't exist. There, I critique various arguments for serious actualism and serious presentism. In Chapter 3, I consider the utility of being an actualist who accepts the independence thesis. I show that there are many problems in metaphysics, philosophy of religion, and philosophy of language that may be addressed by adopting independence actualism. In Chapter 4, I consider the principal reasons that have led people to adopt Meinongianism. I argue that the independence actualist may account for all the metaphysical data that the Meinongian may account for. In Chapter 5, I consider the semantics of "exists" and ask whether it is a first- or second-order predicate. I argue that the independence actualist has room to claim it is a first-order predicate. In Chapter 6, I examine the question of the dependence of singular propositions and haecceities on objects they are about ("existentialism"). In

Chapter 7, I consider two sorts of Meinongianism, what I call *Robust* and *Deflationary* Meinongianism. The distinction between the two has to do with the sorts of properties the Meinongian thinks nonexistent objects have. I argue that if one is not convinced by the arguments of the first six chapters and one remains committed to Meinongianism, one ought to be a Robust Meinongian. In Chapter 8, I consider the relation between God and other necessarily existing entities; in particular, whether we should say that God grounds the existence of necessarily existing abstracta.

I want to say a bit about the metaphysical and metaphilosophical underpinnings of the book. I assume a metaphysics similar to that found in Plantinga (1974): There are abundant properties, relations, states of affairs, and propositions, and they are not reducible to one another. Possible worlds are maximal states of affairs or propositions. Propositions and states of affairs are structured entities with properties, relations, and concrete individuals as constituents. (This last part runs contrary to Plantinga; I discuss this in Chapter 6.) There are also haecceities, properties like *being identical with Socrates*. I help myself to this metaphysical background not only because I find it plausible but also because I think it's explanatorily useful.

I also don't think it's at all *obvious* that what I say in the book is true. This is because I don't find very much in philosophy, much less abstract metaphysics, obvious. I am very aware that on any issue in abstract metaphysics one likes, there are really smart and capable philosophers who disagree. There are really smart and capable philosophers who disagree with most everything I say in the course of this book. Furthermore, I don't think I'm much better situated epistemically than they are. As a result, I have an aversion to pounding on the table while claiming an obvious *reductio* of some view and similar dialectical maneuvers. Why write the book then? Because I find the arguments in it convincing, and in giving philosophical arguments, we get a better sense of the logical space of various metaphysical debates. In this way philosophy progresses.[1]

1

Independence Actualism Explicated

This book is an exploration of the metaphysics of existence and nonexistence, primarily through the lens of independence actualism. Independence actualism is the conjunction of two theses:

1. **The Independence Thesis**: Objects may exemplify properties and stand in relations at worlds and at times where they don't exist.
2. **Actualism**: Necessarily, whatever there is, exists.

In subsequent chapters I will defend both the independence thesis apart from independence actualism and actualism by way of defending independence actualism. Immediately, though, I want to note two things about our definition of actualism. First, if actualism so-conceived is true, there aren't any of the sorts of objects that Meinong is famous for believing in; there are no golden mountains or round squares or the like. Second, in stating actualism, we are able to make sense of the notion of quantification beyond existential quantification. When we formulate actualism, we're saying something like the following: Consider golden mountains, round squares, and Noman (Salmon 1987)—there *aren't* any of those things. We aren't simply saying they don't exist. Meinong agrees that they don't exist (and we don't want to class him as an actualist). Rather, we're saying that there aren't, in a maximally wide sense, things like golden mountains, round squares, or Noman. There is nothing beyond that which exists; nor could there be.

While giving initial definitions, we also should define *Meinongianism*. Meinongianism is the thesis that there are or could be things that don't exist. Or, Meinongianism is the claim that in the scope of our widest quantifiers are (or could be) nonexistent objects. Thus, Meinongianism is the denial of actualism.[1]

Some people (e.g., Lycan 1979, 1994) have objected that quantification beyond existential quantification doesn't make any sense—that it's "literally gibberish." I don't know how to convince such a person that what I'm saying here makes sense. *I* think it makes sense. I think that Meinongians have a coherent view, even if I think it's false.

Peter van Inwagen provides an argument that Meinongian theories are incoherent.

> And, of course, if there is no distinction in meaning between "be" and "exist," then neo Meinongianism cannot be stated without contradiction. If "be" and "exist" mean the same thing, then the open sentence "x exists" is equivalent to "$\exists y(x=y)$." And, if that is so, "There are objects that do not exist" is logically equivalent to "Something is not identical with itself." Since neo-Meinongians obviously do not mean to embrace a contradiction, their theory depends on the premise that "exist" means something other than "be." But, so far as I can see, there is nothing for "exists" *to* mean but "be." In the absence of further explanation, I am therefore inclined to reject their theory as meaningless. (van Inwagen 2014b, ch. 8, pp. 172–3)

The "neo-Meinongian" that van Inwagen has in mind is Terrence Parsons (1980). Van Inwagen claims that Meinongians like Parsons follow early Russell (1903) in saying that nonexistent objects have being, and thus that being is not the same as existence. Many Meinongians—Meinong included—think that at least some nonexistent objects also lack being. Parsons himself (1980, pp. 10–11) claims to be agnostic on whether nonexistent objects all have being. In the above argument, van Inwagen argues that the Meinongian *must* adopt the view that being is distinct from existence on pain of incoherence and states further that being can't, after all, be distinct from existence. Is this an argument that should worry the Meinongian?

Van Inwagen argues that if "be" and "exist" mean the same thing, then "x exists" means the same thing as "$\exists y(x=y)$." The latter, however, just means that x is identical with itself. So in claiming there could be objects that don't exist, one is admitting of the possibility of there being objects that are not identical with themselves. This is, of course, bad. However, I don't think that van Inwagen reads the Meinongian's quantifiers properly in this argument. Someone like Parsons will say that the sentence, "There are objects that don't exist" is true and that the quantification in the first part of the sentence is wider than existential quantification. If we consider some randomly chosen nonexistent object x, it will be true that $\sim(\exists y(x=y))$. That is, it will be true that x is not identical with any existing object. But the Meinongian isn't thereby committed to saying that x isn't identical with itself. Someone like Parsons may contend that the sentence, "There is a y such that x=y" is true, where the quantifier in the sentence is a broader, Meinongian quantifier that ranges over existent and nonexistent objects.

In giving this reply to van Inwagen, we haven't said anything about the semantics of "being" or "existence." We have relied on a quantifier broader than the existential quantifier. But if the Meinongian isn't allowed that, then her view really is incoherent and nonsensical.

Thus, I don't think that van Inwagen shows that there is a problem with the Meinongian's claiming that being=existence. Indeed, were I to be a Meinongian, I'd be one who claims that being=existence, and thus that nonexistent objects were also beyond being. I think that it is actually really difficult to show that there is something rotten at the core of Meinongianism, even if one rejects it, as I do.

There are two things I want to accomplish in the rest of this first chapter. First, I want to say something about the conception of actualism with which I am working. In particular, I want to say why I choose it over competing conceptions. Second, I want to make the case that independence actualism is in fact actualism.

1.1 About Actualism

There are multiple conceptions of actualism in the philosophical literature. I want to note some of the different ways "actualism" is used and say something about why I prefer the conception I do.

"Actualism" first gained currency in something like its current sense as a result of Robert Adams's "Theories of Actuality" from 1974 (Adams 1974).[2] In that paper, Adams defines actualism as follows:

> Actualism, with respect to possible worlds, is the view that if there are any true statements in which there are said to be nonactual possible worlds, they must be reducible to statements in which the only things there are said to be are things which there are in the actual world and which are not identical with nonactual possibles. (Adams 1974, p. 224)

Thus, actualism begins its life as a claim about grounding or truthmaking. Let's mark this first conception of the term.

Actualism$_T$: True claims about nonactual possible worlds are made true by existing things in the actual world.

In 1976, we find Alvin Plantinga saying in "Actualism and Possible Worlds," "Suppose we follow Robert Adams in using the name 'Actualism' to designate the view that there neither are nor could be any nonexistent objects" (Plantinga 2003a, p. 106). This, of course, *isn't* Adams's concept of actualism. But it is a perfectly good concept, so let's note it.

Actualism$_P$: There aren't, nor could there have been nonexistent entities.
(Equivalently, necessarily, whatever there is, exists.)

Plantinga himself maintains this conception of actualism throughout his career.

> "Actualism, as I shall construe it is the view that there neither are nor could be nonexistent objects." (Plantinga 1979, p. 145)

> "I follow Robert Adams in using 'actualism' to name the claim that there neither are nor could have been things that do not exist—the claim that the proposition there are no things that do not exist is necessarily true." (Plantinga 1985a, p. 314)

Other philosophers use the term the way Plantinga does (Bergmann 1996; Crisp 2005).

In 1981 in his other seminal paper on actualism, "Actualism and Thisness," we find Adams saying, "Actualism is the doctrine that there are no things that do not exist in the actual world."[3] In the years after Adams's 1981 paper, we may observe a number of other authors defining actualism using "actual" in the definition. Here are four.

> "However, I am an actualist. I deny that there are any mere *possibilia*, and instead insist that everything that exists actually exists." (Karen Bennett 2006)

> "Actualism is the thesis that everything there is, i.e., everything that exists, is actual." (Michael Nelson and Edward Zalta 2009)

> "I am an actualist. I think that whatever exists—whatever has being in any sense—is actual." (Christopher Menzel 1990)

"Actualism is the metaphysical position that everything that exists, exists at the actual world." (G. W. Fitch 1996)

From these, we can note another conception of actualism, one that has "actual" in the definition.

Actualism$_A$: Everything that exists is actual.

If one examines the literature, one can find other, subtly different definitions from the several we have described thus far. One might, upon seeing these different conceptions of actualism, conclude that there is some sort of confusion in the concept that makes it not worth studying (Williamson 2013). I think this isn't the case, though. Even if we haven't settled on a definition of "actualism," there are several concepts here that I think are worth considering.

As the reader has already seen, I am calling Actualism$_P$ actualism *simpliciter*. I do this for three reasons. First, I like the way it categorizes figures in the metaphysics of existence and nonexistence. According to Actualism$_P$, early Russell and Meinong are not actualists; later Russell is. Richard Routley (2018) and Terrence Parsons (1980) are not actualists; Plantinga, Adams, and Quine are. David Lewis (1986) is an actualist, which seems right to me—Lewis doesn't think there are the sorts of entities that Meinong, Routley, and Parsons believe in. Linsky and Zalta (1994, 1996) are actualists, as they insist.[4]

Second, I have concerns about the other views and how they map onto representative philosophical debates. Consider our first definition of actualism:

Actualism$_T$: True claims about nonactual possible worlds are made true by existing things in the actual world.

If we consider the seminal debate in the field—that between later Russell and Meinong—and we're trying to track that debate with "actualism," we could do better than Actualism$_T$. To see this, suppose I think there are nonexistent objects (suppose there is one), but they don't play any role in grounding claims about nonactual possible worlds. So, perhaps I have Plantinga's modal metaphysics with analyses of claims about other possible worlds in terms of actually existing abstract worlds. But in addition to this, I think there is an object which doesn't exist. Then I could be an actualist in the sense of Actualism$_T$. But I'm not an actualist if I believe in nonexistent objects, at least not in the sense that later Russell, Quine, and Plantinga are. This of course isn't to say that the concept in Actualism$_T$ is illegitimate or isn't worth exploring. It's just to say that it doesn't get actualism right, if what we're after is categorizing properly historical philosophical debates.

Or consider our third definition of actualism:

Actualism$_A$: Everything that exists is actual.

With Actualism$_A$ we have a term in the definition that is missing from Actualism$_P$—"actual." But the semantics of "actual" are tricky. As someone who accepts Actualism$_P$, I'm inclined to say that what is actual is what exists and what exists is primitive. This seems right to me; it seems that existence is the more basic concept here. (Though by taking Actualism$_P$ to be actualism, I don't need to give an analysis of "actual" just in virtue of stating the definition of actualism.) But with Actualism$_A$ the analysis of actuality in terms of existence can't work on pain of making the definition trivial. Should we analyze "actual" indexically à la David Lewis (1970, 1973, 1986)? That won't do for the actualist, as it's too weak a conception. It doesn't get at the actualist's real metaphysical distinction between the actual world and other merely possible worlds. Indeed, every world is actual relative to itself in the indexical sense. Overall, the analysis of "actual" is tricky (see van Inwagen 2012); it is best to avoid it in our characterization of actualism, if we can.

Further, suppose I think that there are nonexistent *possibilia*. But I think that everything that *exists* is actual. Then I'm an actualist in the sense of Actualism$_A$. But if we're tracking the concept in the debate between Russell and Meinong, I'm not an actualist. As before, I'm not an actualist if I believe in nonexistent objects. So there is an important way in which Actualism$_A$ fails to get at what we're after in a definition of actualism, if what we're after is properly categorizing historical philosophical debates.

The third reason why I take Actualism$_P$ to be actualism *simpliciter* is that my use of "actualism" is in keeping with important uses—both early and later on—of the term. Plantinga is one of the principal defenders of actualism in the last half century, and I regard myself in good company with him.

But, at the end of the day, I'm not super-concerned about this semantic debate. If someone else insists that some other conception of actualism that isn't (or isn't equivalent to) Actualism$_P$ is *the* correct use of the term, then fine. I'm happy to call the principal view explored in the book *Independence*

Actualism$_p$ and proceed from there. There clearly is an important concept that Actualism$_p$ gets at, whatever we call it. But I think that the justification for my rendering of Actualism$_p$ as actualism *simpliciter* is strong, and I will proceed as though actualism is Actualism$_p$.

1.2 Is It Actualism?

So we have a conception of actualism. Is it possible to have an actualist theory that allows objects that don't exist to have properties and stand in relations? Why isn't that a Meinongian theory? What's the difference between independence actualism and full-blooded Meinongianism?

Some have been skeptical of a theory like independence actualism, arguing that any theory that allows things that don't exist to exemplify properties and stand in relations is *ipso facto* a Meinongian theory. Mark Hinchliff, who has long championed the idea that one can reply to problems with presentism by countenancing non-present objects that exemplify properties, is one person who is skeptical of this sort of idea. In Hinchliff (1988), he says:

> I find this ... strategy [where one allows objects to have properties and stand in relations, but doesn't embrace Meinongianism] to be an evasion. Once we say that nonexistent objects (plural quantifier) have properties, or say that nonexistent objects are in the extensions of some predicates, we are already unofficially quantifying over nonexistent objects. It is then just an evasion not to quantify over nonexistent objects. (p. 108)

However, I don't see why we should think that this is true. As a way to see this, consider the difference between free logics and Meinongian logics. We note the following definition of free logic from Ermanno Bencivenga in the *Handbook of Philosophical Logic*, 2nd ed.:

> A free logic is a formal system of quantification theory, with or without identity, which allows for some singular terms in in some circumstances to be thought as denoting no existing objects, and in which quantifiers are invariably thought of as having existential import. (Bencivenga 2002, pp. 148–9)

Nino B. Cocchiarella says something similar about free logic:

> A first-order logic of existence should allow for the possibility that some of our singular terms might fail to denote an existent object, which, according to actualism, is only to say that those singular terms are denotationless rather than that what they denote are objects (beings) that do not exist. Such a logic for actualism amounts to what nowadays is called a *free logic*. (Cocchiarella 1991, p. 243; emphasis in the original)

And Karel Lambert, the originator of the term "free logic," says, "[N]o free logician shares Meinong's world picture" (Lambert 1983, p. 122).[5]

Compare free logic to Meinongian logic. Jacek Paśniczek gives four characteristics of a Meinongian logic:

> a) Meinongian logics assume an ontology of non-existent objects … [and] the objects are quantified over in the logics.
> b) Meinongian logics stipulate two modes of predication (Zalta) or two kinds of properties (Parsons).
> c) Meinongian logics are bivalent.
> d) Meinongian logics are second-order intensional logics ("intensional" means, amongst other things, that propositions, properties and relations are not reducible to their extensions). (Paśniczek 2001, pp. 227–8)

A natural way to understand the difference between free and Meinongian logics involves noting the reach of the quantifiers in the different systems. Free logics often involve an inner and an outer domain of objects, with quantifiers ranging over the inner domain. The outer domain objects still do work in making predications true (at least in positive free logics), even though quantifiers don't range over these objects. Contrast free logic with Meinongian logic: In a Meinongian logic the objects in the outer domain will be quantified over with a broader, Meinongian quantifier.

This distinction between free and Meinongian logics maps on to the distinction between Meinongianism and independence actualism. Both Meinongianism and independence actualism involve objects beyond the range of our existential quantifiers that exemplify properties and stand in relations. However, only the Meinongian has a broader, Meinongian quantifier under which objects that don't fall under our existential quantifiers fall. For the independence actualist, our broadest quantifier is the existential quantifier.

The core of independence actualism is that objects that don't fall under the broadest actualist quantifier may nevertheless exemplify properties and stand in relations.

Plantinga calls "serious actualism" the view that necessarily no object has a property in a world in which it doesn't exist (Plantinga 2003b, p. 179). (We will consider Plantinga's serious actualism further in Chapter 2.) One might think that once one gives up serious actualism, one gives up actualism. But it's striking that many philosophers have denied serious actualism without thinking of themselves as Meinongians. Indeed, Plantinga himself humorously suggests the name "frivolous actualism" for "the conjunction of actualism with the denial of serious actualism" (Plantinga 2003b, p. 179). Importantly, frivolous actualism is an *actualist* view rather than a Meinongian view. For a frivolous actualist (i.e., an independence actualist!), there are no nonexistent objects in the scope of their widest quantifiers.

I contend there is conceptual room, then, between serious actualism and Meinongianism. Independence actualism inhabits this room between the two views: maintaining with actualism that necessarily, there are no nonexistent objects, and maintaining with Meinongianism that objects that don't exist may exemplify properties and stand in relations.

Independence actualism is the lens through which we will consider a wide number of issues in the metaphysics of existence and nonexistence in the course of the book. It seems to me that one can solve a great many philosophical problems with independence actualism, without being a Meinongian. And why would one accept nonexistent entities into one's ontology unless absolutely necessary?

2

The Independence Thesis

In Chapter 1, we investigated the concept of actualism and the coherence of a non-Meinongian acceptance of the independence thesis:

The Independence Thesis: Objects may exemplify properties and stand in relations at worlds and at times where they don't exist.

In this chapter we will examine the independence thesis itself. We will consider arguments against it and for it. We also will consider different proposals about which sorts of properties and relations may be had by things though those things don't exist.

2.1 Arguments against the Independence Thesis: Arguments for Serious Actualism

In the history of philosophy, there are many people who have thought the independence thesis obviously false. For instance, we find Malebranche in the beginning of his *Dialogues on Metaphysics* (Malebranche 1992, p. 149) asserting, "Nothing has no properties." Leibniz says, "[A] nonentity has no attributes" (quoted in Mates 1986, p. 99). But however obvious these principles seemed to Malebranche and Leibniz, we're after arguments against the independence thesis. Fortunately, we have some to consider.

In the philosophical literature, most of the arguments that tell against a claim like the independence thesis are arguments for what has come to be called serious actualism: No object has a property in a world where it doesn't exist.[1] There also are arguments for its temporal counterpart, serious presentism: No object has a property at a time it doesn't exist.[2] If we had sound arguments for the conjunction of serious actualism and presentism, we would rule out independence actualism as a viable thesis.[3]

Thus, it is important to address arguments for serious actualism and serious presentism if one is considering independence actualism.

In this second section of the chapter, I want to look at what I take to be the principal arguments for serious actualism. In the third I will look at what I take to be the principal arguments for serious presentism. The structure of arguments for serious actualism or presentism typically comes in the form of arguments that they are entailed by actualism or presentism, respectively. I will argue that the extant arguments for each either are not sound or are not cogent, in that they contain premises that one would rationally accept only if one already accepted its conclusion. Either way, the independence thesis is not threatened.

2.1.1 Plantinga's Original Argument for Serious Actualism

In recent metaphysics, the principal defender of the view that objects have properties only if they exist is Alvin Plantinga. We're going to consider carefully his two main arguments for serious actualism here. In a paper in a collection of essays on the work of Roderick Chisholm from 1979 (Plantinga 1979), Alvin Plantinga argues that actualism entails serious actualism.[4]

> Now it may be tempting to suppose that serious actualism is a corollary of actualism *tout court*. For suppose, in accord with actualism, that
>
> (13) There are no nonexistent objects
>
> is necessarily true and hence true in every possible world. Then the same can be said for
>
> (14) For any property P, there are no nonexistent objects that have P
>
> that is
>
> (15) Whatever has P, exists.
>
> Now consider Socrates, and let P be any property and W be any world in which Socrates has P. Then
>
> (16) Socrates has P
>
> is true in W; since (15) is also true in W, so is
>
> (17) Socrates exists.
>
> But then it follows that if Socrates has a property P in a world W, Socrates exists in W; and of course the same goes for everything else. (Plantinga 1983, pp. 11–12; emphasis in the original)

We can see pretty quickly that this is not an argument the premises of which anyone who accepts independence actualism would find compelling. (13) is necessarily true if actualism is true. (14) is also necessarily true given actualism as well. But the inference from (14) to (15) is not at all obviously valid and is not one that any actualist who isn't already a serious actualist would accept. It can be true in W that there are no nonexistent objects that have P; nevertheless, the defender of the independence actualism will maintain that there still can be things that in W exemplify P though they don't exist in W. The independence actualist's thesis is that there can be objects that exemplify properties at worlds and times where they don't exist, even though there are no nonexistent objects in the scope of our widest quantifiers. In particular, the independence actualist rejects the inference from *x has F in W* to either *x exists in W* or *x is a nonexistent object in W*. If I'm a Meinongian or serious actualist, this looks like a good inference. But it is precisely the inference that the independence actualist wants to reject. So this argument won't serve as a non-question-begging argument against the independence actualist.

By 1983, Plantinga himself had given up this argument. In "On Existentialism," he says,

> Now I said it was tempting thus to infer serious actualism from actualism; but the above argument represents at best a bit of flocculent thinking. We can see this as follows. If actualism is true, then
>
> (18) Whatever does *not* exist, exists
>
> is true in every possible world; few would be tempted to infer, however, that if Socrates does not exist in a world *W**, then he exists in that world. The trouble with the argument, obviously, is the following: (15) is indeed true in W, as is (16). To infer that (17) is true in W, however, we must suppose that
>
> (19) If Socrates has P, then Socrates exists
>
> is also true there. One thinks of (19) as following from (15) by Universal Instantiation. (15) says that everything there is—everything that exists and everything else as well, if there is anything else—has a certain property: *being such that if it has P, then it exists*. (19) (construed *de re* as *Socrates is such that if he has P then he exists*) says just that Socrates has the property (15) says everything there is has. But then clearly (19) doesn't follow from (15) alone. Another premiss is needed: the premiss that Socrates is one of the things there are. Of course this premiss is true in fact, but perhaps it isn't

true in *W*. So from the fact that (15) is true in W we cannot properly infer that (19) is also true in *W*. (Plantinga 1983, p. 12)

This is a different strategy for criticizing his original 1979 argument than that we just considered. The main objection Plantinga has here is that

(15) Whatever has P, exists

doesn't by itself entail

(19) If Socrates has P, Socrates exists.

And Plantinga says you need (19) to derive (17), which is the end of the proof of serious actualism from actualism.

To see his concern, note that (15) is equivalent to

(15') Necessarily, for any x, if x has P, then x exists.

Plantinga would claim that (15') doesn't entail (19). Consider some arbitrary world W1. At W1 it will be true that if x has P, then x exists. But will it be true if Socrates has P, then Socrates exists? Only if Socrates exists at W1, says Plantinga.

So the worry is that any world you pick where Socrates has P will be one where one can derive that Socrates exists only by calling on a conditional premise that is true only if Socrates exists. The inference from Socrates having P to Socrates thereby existing works only if you antecedently assume Socrates exists.

I think that Plantinga is too hard on his original argument here. If we have

(15) Whatever has P exists

and

(16) Socrates has P

surely we can derive

(17) Socrates exists.

(15) is a necessary truth; it says in any world, if something x has P, x exists. Then it is true in some randomly chosen world W where Socrates has P; that if something has P, it exists. (16) is true in W. So we know Socrates exists in W. W

is randomly chosen, so we know that necessarily given actualism, if Socrates has P, then Socrates exists. So far this seems a perfectly good argument, on the assumption that we have (15).

But don't we need (19) to be true? Well, given that (15) is a necessary truth, (19) won't be false. Why does Plantinga think (19) is true in W only if Socrates exists in W? The only reason I can think of is existentialism, the view that haecceities and singular propositions are dependent on the objects they are about. The existentialist would say that if Socrates doesn't exist in W, (19) isn't true in W; this is because (19) doesn't exist in W if Socrates doesn't exist in W. But of course, the arguments that we're now discussing come in a paper by Plantinga the point of which is a refutation of existentialism. So I don't think it's fair to attribute existentialism to Plantinga as an explanation for there being a question as to the truth of (19) in W. But setting aside existentialism, I don't know why someone (especially Plantinga) would wonder if (19) were true after having established (15).

So I agree with Plantinga that his first argument for the entailment between actualism and serious actualism isn't a good one. There is conceptual room for the independence actualist to deny the inference in it from (14) to (15). But I don't agree with him as to what is wrong with it.

2.1.2 Plantinga's Second Argument for Serious Actualism

Two years after giving the above arguments in "On Existentialism," Plantinga published his conviction that actualism did, after all, entail serious actualism (Plantinga 1985a). His argument for this comes in two parts. First, he argues that necessarily, if actualism is true, nothing exemplifies nonexistence.

> Now first, there is a perfectly straightforward argument from actualism to the conclusion that nonexistence (call it $\bar{E}$) is not exemplified.
>
> Consider
>
> (1) For any property P, if P is exemplified, then there is something that exemplifies P
>
> and
>
> (2) For any property P, whatever exemplifies P exists.

> Here the quantifiers are to be taken as widely as possible; if you think there are things that don't exist, then read the quantifiers as ranging over those things as well as the more conventional existent sort. (1), I take it, is obviously true. (2) is a consequence of actualism, according to which it is necessary that whatever there is, exists. (1) and (2) together entail
>
> > (3) If nonexistence is exemplified, then nonexistence is exemplified by something that exists.
>
> Since the consequent of (3) is clearly (necessarily) false, it is false that nonexistence is exemplified. And since (given the truth of actualism) each of the premises of this argument is necessarily true, it follows that nonexistence is necessarily unexemplified; that nonexistence is not exemplified is a necessary truth. (Plantinga 1985a, pp. 318–19)

He then uses the conclusion that nonexistence can't be exemplified as part of an argument that actualism entails serious actualism.

> It is easy to see, I think, that we can go on to deduce serious actualism from actualism. For suppose an object—Socrates, let's say—exemplifies a property P in a world W. Then (necessarily) if W had been actual, Socrates would have exemplified P. Now (necessarily) if Socrates had exemplified P, then either Socrates would have exemplified $P\&E$, the conjunction of P with existence, or Socrates would have exemplified $P\& \bar{E}$ (where $\bar{E}$ is the complement of existence). As we have just seen, it is impossible that Socrates exemplify $\bar{E}$, and hence impossible that Socrates exemplify $P\& \bar{E}$. It is therefore necessary that if Socrates had exemplified P, then Socrates would have exemplified existence. In terms of possible worlds; suppose Socrates exemplifies P in W. Then either Socrates exemplifies P and existence in W or Socrates exemplifies $P\& \bar{E}$ in W. There is no world in which Socrates exemplifies $P\& \bar{E}$. So Socrates exemplifies existence (that is, exists) in W. (Plantinga 1985a, p. 319)

Let's consider Plantinga's overall argument one part at a time.

I take it the first argument—that *nonexistence* can't be exemplified—proceeds in the following sort of way. If property P is exemplified, then there is something that has P. The only candidates available, given the truth of actualism, are existing things. So the only candidates available for exemplifying *nonexistence* are existing things. But obviously no existing thing can exemplify *nonexistence*. So *nonexistence* can't be exemplified.

There are two replies that one may make to the first part of Plantinga's argument, depending on how one reads (1). On either reading, the argument begs the question against the independence actualist. On the one hand, the independence actualist may say that at a world W where Socrates doesn't exist, there is something that exemplifies P—Socrates. Now, Socrates isn't in the scope of our widest quantifiers at W, but we can point to what exemplifies P at W. Thus, on this reply, the independence actualist will have no quarrel with (1). But (2) will in this case beg the question against the independence actualist. Her view is that things may exemplify properties at worlds where they don't exist; (2) is just a denial of this on this reading. She will insist that (2) isn't a consequence of actualism.

On the other hand (and this is the more natural objection, I think), suppose we read (1) as asserting that if P is exemplified, there is something in the scope of our widest quantifiers that does so. Taken this way, the independence actualist will reject (1), as (1) is a straight-out denial of her view. Only a serious actualist or Meinongian would accept the first premise of Plantinga's argument. We get no argument from Plantinga for it; only that he regards it as obviously true.

Obviously, insofar Plantinga's overall argument for serious actualism here relies on the soundness of the argument for impossibility of the exemplification of *nonexistence*, we know that the overall argument fails. But it is instructive to look at the second part of the overall argument more closely anyway. I take it this second part proceeds as follows. Consider a world W in which Socrates exemplifies P. In W, Socrates exemplifies P & *existence* or P & *nonexistence*. From the previous argument we know that necessarily, nothing exemplifies *nonexistence*. Therefore, in W, Socrates exemplifies P & *existence*. So necessarily, for any property P, if Socrates exemplifies P, Socrates exists. The argument generalizes and yields serious actualism.

In this book we have not yet considered the question of which properties the independence actualist should think of objects that don't exist having. We will do so at the end of the chapter and in subsequent chapters. There are two routes that we could imagine the independence actualist taking in reply to the second part of Plantinga's overall argument. First, she might grant Plantinga's premise that in W Socrates exemplifies either *nonexistence* or *existence*, and she might insist that the disjunction is made true by the fact that Socrates exemplifies *nonexistence*. The rejection of the first part of Plantinga's overall argument opens the way for her to do this. Second, she might insist that

Socrates lacks both *existence* and *nonexistence* in W. Maybe there are various properties that objects that don't exist will lack, and maybe we should think that they have neither these properties nor their complements. There then are two ways that the independence actualist might reply specifically to the second part of Plantinga's second argument for serious actualism.

2.1.3 A New, Straightforward, Plantinga-Inspired Argument for Serious Actualism

One can see the seeds of a much more straightforward argument for serious actualism in Plantinga's overall argument from the last section. It proceeds as follows:

1. Necessarily, for any property F and world W; if F is exemplified in W, there is (in the scope of our maximally wide quantifiers) something x that exemplifies F in W.
2. Necessarily, the only things in the scope of our widest quantifiers are existing things (from actualism).
3. Therefore, necessarily, for any property F and world W; if F is exemplified in W, F is exemplified by something that exists in W (serious actualism).

So, if a property is exemplified, it is exemplified by something in the scope of our widest quantifiers. Given the truth of actualism, our quantifiers are actualist. Thus, necessarily, properties are exemplified only by existing things.

We can see from our above reply to Plantinga's second argument for serious actualism how the independence actualist will reject this argument. Central to the independence actualist's view is that (1) is false; things can exemplify properties even though they neither exist nor are nonexistent objects that fall under Meinongian quantifiers. So, absent an argument for (1) (and it's very hard to see how a non-question-begging argument for (1) can be given), the independence actualist is well within her rights to reject it.

2.1.4 Bergmann's "New Argument" for Serious Actualism

In Bergmann (1996, 1999), Michael Bergmann gives a new argument for the proposition that actualism entails serious actualism. Hudson (1997) criticizes Bergmann's argument, and Bergmann replies to Hudson in Bergmann (1999).

In this section, I want to consider Bergmann's 1996 argument and the exchange between Hudson and Bergmann about it.

Bergmann (1996) begins by noting the counterexample usually given against serious actualism—that objects exemplify *nonexistence* in worlds they don't exist. Bergmann argues that those who endorse this counterexample to serious actualism are committed to the possibility of *transworld property exemplification*. Of this concept Bergmann says, "[Transworld property exemplification] occurs when a property is exemplified in a world w, not by an object that is in w (i.e., has being in w) but by an object that is in another world w*" (Bergmann 1996, p. 357). Bergmann argues that transworld property exemplification is impossible. Thus, he argues that the counterexample to serious actualism from the claim that Socrates exemplifies *nonexistence* in worlds where he doesn't exist fails.

Bergmann begins by arguing that the actualist who denies serious actualism is committed to the possible truth of transworld property exemplification. He formalizes the possibility of transworld property exemplification:

(3) ◊ ∃x ∃w ∃p [(x exemplifies p in w) & ~(x is in w)].⁵

He then notes the denial of (3)

(4) □ ∀x ∀w ∀p [(x exemplifies p in w) →(x is in w)]

conjoined with (5), which follows from actualism

(5) □ ∀x ∀w [(x is in w) →(x exists in w)]

yields serious actualism:

(6) □ ∀x ∀w ∀p [(x exemplifies p in w) →(x exists in w)].

Thus, the person who accepts actualism but not serious actualism is committed to transworld property exemplification. He then argues that transworld property exemplification is impossible. The argument proceeds as follows.

Suppose, for *reductio*, that transworld property exemplification is possible, viz.,

(3) ◊ ∃x ∃w ∃p [(x exemplifies p in w) & ~(x is in w)].

then

(7) ∃w ∃p (It is true in w that there is an instance of p being exemplified but not by anything in w).

He takes the following to be a truism:

> (8) ∀w (It is true in w that there is nothing except what there is in w)

(7) and (8) entail

> (9) ∃w ∃p (It is true in w that there is an instance of p being exemplified but not by anything at all).

(9) contradicts

> (10) Necessarily, every instance of property exemplification is an instance of a property being exemplified by something.

He continues, "Since (10) is obviously true, (9) is false. And since (3) implies (9), (3) is also false."

What should we make of Bergmann's overall argument here? On the face of it, his argument, though couched in much more formalism, resembles the argument in the last section. If we affirm actualism and deny serious actualism, then we are committed to there being instances of property exemplification where there is nothing at all that exemplifies the property. But this is absurd, so we should be serious actualists if actualists.

Earlier we saw that there were two ways one could take the first premise in Plantinga's second argument for serious actualism. Similarly, there are two ways in which we can take Bergmann's (10). The most natural way is to think of it the way we thought of the first premise of the argument in Plantinga-inspired argument of the last section:

> (1) Necessarily, for any property F and world W; if F is exemplified in W, there is (in the scope of our maximally-wide quantifiers) something x that exemplifies F in W.

We took this premise to say that for every property exemplification, there is something in the scope of our maximally broad quantifiers at W that exemplifies the property. We noted that this is a straight-out denial of independence actualism. Bergmann's (10) could be read as asserting the same sort of claim: Necessarily, every instance of property exemplification is by something that is in the scope of our broadest quantifiers. This also will be rejected by the independence actualist as a mere denial of her theory.

There is another way to take (10) as well. Suppose I'm an independence actualist who takes Socrates to have a property F at a world W where Socrates doesn't exist. Why can't I say in reply to Bergmann, "You want to know what exemplifies F in W? It's Socrates. So F is exemplified by something. Now, it's not anything in the scope of our widest quantifiers at W. But we can point to what exemplifies F in W." With this sort of reply the independence actualist is rejecting Bergmann's (8) and (9).

It is my suspicion that Bergmann intends his (10) in the former way so that the argument resembles the argument for serious actualism in the last section. If so, our reply to his argument then would mirror the reply to that argument.

Hudson (1997) gives a reconstruction of Bergmann's argument in which he also takes Bergmann to be doing something very close to begging the question against the actualist who denies serious actualism (i.e., the independence actualist). Bergmann (1999) claims that Hudson gets his argument wrong. Their disagreement centers on Hudson's taking Hudson's principle

(OT)* Necessarily, every instance of property exemplification is an instance of a property being exemplified by something ... that is in the world in which the property is being exemplified.

to be equivalent to Bergmann's

(10) Necessarily, every instance of property exemplification is an instance of a property being exemplified by something.

Hudson claims that Bergmann relies on the obviousness of (OT)*. Bergmann insists, rather, he relies on the obviousness of (10). Clearly the two principles are different, as Bergmann says. For (OT)* isn't open to the two readings (10) is. If we consider a world W where Socrates doesn't exist and yet exemplifies F, we have a clear counterexample to (OT)*. But, as we saw in our second interpretation of Bergmann's argument, there is room for the independence actualist to claim that (10) is satisfied. So it seems to me that Bergmann is right about Hudson misconstruing his argument, though Hudson may be right about the sort of problem Bergmann's argument suffers from (something close to begging the question).

2.1.5 Bergmann's Newest Argument for Serious Actualism

In light of Hudson's criticisms, Bergmann (1999) formulates an argument for the entailment of serious actualism by actualism in a different manner.

It proceeds as follows. Assume for *reductio* that transworld property exemplification is possible:

a) ◊ ∃x ∃w ∃p [(x exemplifies p in w) & ~(x is in w)].

(a) entails

b) (Result)*$_{New}$ ∃w ∃p (It is true in w that there is an instance of p being exemplified by something but not by anything in w)

the following is a truism

c) ∀w (It is true in w that there is nothing except what there is in w)

from (a)-(c) we get

d) (Result)$_{New}$ ∃w ∃p (It is true in w that there is an instance of p being exemplified by something but not by anything at all).

(d) is a contradiction, Bergmann says. Thus, he claims he doesn't need to rely on something like (9)'s contradicting what he takes to be an obvious truth with (10), as he did in his original argument.

But (d), properly understood, isn't contradictory. To see this, consider again our world W where Socrates doesn't exist but exemplifies F. In W, F is exemplified by something—Socrates, but (let us say) not by anything in the scope of our widest quantifiers at that world. So one could say that it's a case where F is exemplified by something but not by anything at all. But, I'd put it slightly less tendentiously as being a case where F is exemplified by something but not by anything in the scope of our widest quantifiers at W. That's not contradictory, or at least not obviously so. Once we understand properly the allegedly problematic proposition in Bergmann's newest argument, we see that it's awfully close to a statement of the independence actualist's view.

To see what has gone wrong here, imagine someone claiming the Meinongian contradicts herself. "You say there are things that don't exist. But that's contradictory! How can there exist things that don't exist?" The Meinongian will say,

> You're not understanding the quantifier 'there are' appropriately. It's not an existential quantifier. I'm not saying there exist things that don't exist; of course that would be contradictory. Rather, the quantifier in 'there are' when I say 'there are things that don't exist' is a wider quantifier than the existential quantifier. So when you understand the sentence properly, there is no contradiction in my saying there are things that don't exist.

Something similar has gone wrong with Bergmann's newest argument. Bergmann claims that

(Result)$_{New}$ ∃w ∃p (It is true in w that there is an instance of p being exemplified by something but not by anything at all)

is contradictory. As with the dialogue in the paragraph above, there is a way of taking it so that it is contradictory. But understood as the independence actualist understands it, it's not (or not obviously) contradictory. Indeed, it's the independence actualist main thesis.[6]

2.1.6 Stephanou's Coextensiveness Argument

Yannis Stephanou (2007) gives several arguments for serious actualism, the strongest two of which I want to consider here. The first alleges that the actualist who denies serious actualism (i.e., the independence actualist) isn't able to capture what it is for two properties to be coextensive (Stephanou 2007, pp. 228–9).[7]

1. Assume for *reductio* that for some being x and some property ɸ it is possible that x not exist but exemplify ɸ.
2. Necessarily, every being exists (from actualism).
3. Therefore, necessarily, for any y; if y has ɸ, then y has ɸ and exists (from 2).

   Let the property ɸ' be that of having ɸ and existing.

4. Necessarily, every being that exemplifies ɸ and exists exemplifies ɸ' (from definition of property ɸ').
5. Necessarily, everything that exemplifies ɸ' exemplifies ɸ (obvious).[8]
6. Therefore, necessarily for any y, y has ɸ iff y has ɸ' (3–5).
7. ɸ and ɸ' are coextensive (6).
8. It is possible that x have ɸ, not exist, and lack ɸ' (1, definition of ɸ').
9. ɸ and ɸ' are not coextensive (8).
10. It's not possible for some being x and some property ɸ that x not exist but exemplify ɸ (1–9, *reductio*).

Is this argument one that should worry the independence actualist? I don't believe so. There is a flaw in this argument that is similar to the flaws in other arguments for serious actualism that we've considered in this chapter. Why should the independence actualist grant that (3) follows from (2)? The argument assumes that it follows from actualism that if x has ϕ, x exists and has ϕ. But this is to foreclose on the possibility of independence actualism from the outset. It begs the question against the independence actualist. So this argument for serious actualism isn't a cogent argument against independence actualism.

2.1.7 Stephanou's Plantinga-Like Argument

Stephanou gives another argument that "bears some similarities to Plantinga's [argument considered above in Section 2.1.2]" (Stephanou 2007, p. 237). It proceeds as follows.

Take any being x and any property ϕ.

1. Necessarily, if x exemplifies ϕ, x exemplifies being self-identical.
2. Necessarily, if x exemplifies being self-identical, x also exemplifies being identical with x.
3. It is possible that x exemplify ϕ and not exist (assumption for *reductio*).
4. It is possible that x not exist and have the property being identical with x (1–3).
5. Necessarily, for every property F, if x exemplifies F, then F is exemplified by x and thus F is exemplified (intuitively obvious).
6. Necessarily, for every property F, if F is exemplified, then F is exemplified by something and so something exemplifies F (intuitively obvious).
7. It is possible x not exist and something have the property being identical with x (4–6).
8. It is possible nothing be identical with x and something be identical with x (7).
9. Therefore, 3 is false and serious actualism is true (1–8, *reductio*).

I don't think that Stephanou's second argument is a problem for the independence actualist. The first five premises look unobjectionable to me. But when we get to (6), problems emerge. The independence actualist's view is that properties can be had by objects at worlds where they don't exist. Furthermore, at those worlds, the object isn't a nonexistent object. It isn't in the scope of our widest quantifiers at all. Therefore, it can be that a property F is exemplified and there be nothing that exemplifies it. Thus, (6) is a straight-out denial of the independence actualist's thesis, and she is well within her rights in rejecting it. In this regard, this argument does indeed resemble Plantinga's argument in Section 2.1.2.

So I think we can see that none of the principal arguments for serious actualism are compelling such that the independence actualist ought to give up her view. We turn now to the principal arguments for serious presentism.

2.2 Arguments against the Independence Thesis: Arguments for Serious Presentism

There are fewer discussions of serious presentism than of serious actualism in the philosophical literature. But there are arguments for it. We will consider some of those now. We will see that strategies employed previously for replying to arguments for serious actualism will be useful in replying to them.

2.2.1 Bergmann's Argument for Serious Presentism

In the last part of Bergmann (1999), Michael Bergmann gives an argument that presentism entails serious presentism. Structurally his argument is a temporal analogue of his "newest argument" for serious actualism that we just discussed in Section 2.1.5. The key premise in the argument that presentism entails serious presentism is a principle like (Result)$_{New}$:

(Result-P)$_{New}$ $\lozenge \exists t \exists p$ (It is true that there is an instance of p being exemplified by something, but not by anything at all.)

Bergmann takes (Result-P)$_{New}$ to be contradictory. But as with (Result)$_{New}$, properly understood we can see that (Result-P)$_{New}$ isn't contradictory. What the independence actualist may embrace is a reading of (Result-P)$_{New}$ where there is a time t and a property p such that something exemplifies p at t, but the thing that exemplifies p isn't in the scope of our widest quantifiers at t. Put this way, of course, this is precisely the sort of thing that the independence actualist claims may happen as part of her view. Our reply here, then, mirrors our reply to Bergmann's newest argument mentioned earlier.

2.2.2 Davidson's Argument for Serious Presentism

In Davidson (2003b), I give an argument that presentism entails serious presentism.

1. Necessarily, for any time t, whatever there is (in as temporally neutral sense as one likes) exists at t (presentism).
2. Necessarily, for any property F or relation R and time t, if F or R is exemplified at t, there is/are (in as temporally neutral a sense as one likes) something or things that exemplifies or exemplify F or R at t.
3. Therefore, necessarily, for any property F or relation R and time t, if F or R is exemplified at t, then F or R is exemplified by something or some things that exists or exist at t.
4. Therefore, necessarily, objects exemplify properties or stand in relations at a time only if they exist at that time.

We can see immediately the problem with this argument. It is the temporal analogue of the "straightforward" argument for serious actualism above in Section 2.1.3. There we noted that the independence actualist has no reason to accept the first premise of that argument:

1. Necessarily, for any property F and world W; if F is exemplified in W, there is (in a maximally broad sense so as to range over existent objects and nonexistent objects) something x that exemplifies F in W.

(1) in the earlier argument is precisely what the independence actualist denies is true. Her view is that there are properties that are exemplified but not by anything that is in the scope of our widest quantifiers. The independence actualist will have the same sort of objection to this argument for serious presentism. It is precisely the contention of the independence actualist that there can be properties exemplified at times where there isn't anything in the scope of our widest quantifiers at those times that exemplifies them. So without further argument for Premise 2, the independence actualist is well within her rights to reject it.

2.2.3 Arthur Prior's Arguments in Defense of Serious Presentism

Arthur Prior (1957) gives criticisms of those who affirm presentism though deny serious presentism. His first objection is that there is no difference between a view on which past and future things have properties and don't exist, and a view on which past and future objects have properties and do exist.

> Where x stands for a proper name, it seems to me that the form "x exists" must be logically equivalent to and definable as "there are facts about x" ... If there are facts about x, I cannot see what further fact about x would consist in its existing. (Prior 1957, p. 31)

One further fact, of course, would be that there was something in the scope of the existential quantifier. And this is a significant further fact. Another possible further fact may rest in the proposition that past or future objects (for the presentist independence actualist) may not be complete in their properties. Adding *existence* would then "complete" the object. As we will discuss later in the chapter, there are various options for properties that one might think an object has at worlds and times where it doesn't exist. I suspect the picture that Prior has here is that we begin with a complete, existing past or future object and then we take away just its existence. But it may be that if we take away its existence we take away other properties as well.

Immediately after giving this objection, Prior gives another objection related to the first. He says, "And when x no longer exists or does not yet exist, but there are nevertheless facts about x now, I do not know what the present-tense facts about x would be. Is this dead or unborn man now blue-eyed for example?" (Prior 1957, p. 31). This is an important question. If I say that objects may have properties or stand in relations, though they don't exist, which properties may they have and relations may they stand in? We will consider this question at the end of this chapter and in subsequent chapters.

2.3 Arguments for the Independence Thesis

2.3.1 Takashi Yagisawa's Iterative Argument

In Yagisawa (2005), Takashi Yagisawa gives an argument that serious actualism is false and objects may have properties in worlds where they don't exist. He bases his argument on a principle about iterated modalities:

> (R) For every x, for every property F, for every possible world w1 and w2, x has F at w1 at w2 iff x has F at w1.[9]

To motivate (R), Yagisawa appeals to Plantinga's notion of a world-indexed property (Plantinga 1974, 1978). Plantinga thinks that for each property F that I instantiate actually, I also have the property *having F in α*, where "α" is a name for the actual world. The world-indexed property will be essential to me. If I uniquely exemplify F actually, the world-indexed property will be an individual essence of mine.

To see how Yagisawa's argument goes, suppose Socrates exists in W1 and not W2. Suppose Socrates has F in W1. By (R), Socrates also has F in W1 in W2. Then Socrates has a property in W2, though he doesn't exist there. So serious actualism is false.

Yagisawa says that it is ironic that Plantinga, a serious actualist, says what he says about world-indexed properties. But what Plantinga says about world-indexed properties doesn't entail anything like (R). Plantinga can maintain that I have the property *being the philosopher born at hospital H in year Y in α* in every world in which I exist, without going on to say that I have any properties at all in worlds where I don't exist. Consider some other world where I do exist, W1. In W1 I have the property *being the philosopher born at hospital H in year Y in α*. At another world W2 where I exist, I have the property *having in W1 the property being the philosopher born at hospital H in year Y in α*. And so on for other worlds where I exist. But nothing about this entails that I have any properties at all in a world W3 where I don't exist. Now, if I do have in W2 the second-order property just mentioned, viz., *having in W1 the property being the philosopher born at hospital H in year Y in α*, then I do have a property in W1 (and, according to Plantinga, exist in W1). But having that property in W2 doesn't have any entailments, in Plantinga's thinking, for me in W3.

More generally, I don't see any reason why the serious actualist should accept (R) as a biconditional. Going from left to right will seem fine to the serious actualist. But the entailment from right to left will be rejected without some sort of argument for it, and nothing Plantinga says about indexed essences serves as that argument for Yagisawa.

Yagisawa gives another example to bolster support for (R). He says,

Saul Kripke proposed that Wittgenstein's example

(W) The standard metre stick is one metre long,

is an example of the contingent a priori (Kripke 1980, pp. 54–6, 75–6). Reactions to Kripke's proposal have been mixed but one particular theoretical position is almost universally deemed as untenable, namely, the position which maintains the contingency of (W) while interpreting (W) as saying that the metre stick is one metre long at α (the actual world). The almost universally accepted reason is that if the metre stick is one metre long at α, then for any possible world w, the metre stick is one metre long at α at w, and vice versa. (Yagisawa 2005, p. 40)

It's worth thinking about what a serious actualist like Plantinga would say about this sort of case. Yagisawa says that the proposition

(M) the standard metre stick is 1m long in α

is a necessary truth. Let's grant that. Plantinga would say that M is equivalent to

(M') Necessarily, if the standard metre stick (read rigidly) exists, it is 1m long in α.

But of course that (M') is true doesn't tell us anything about properties the standard metre stick has in a world W1 where it doesn't exist. The proposition (M') is true at W1. But the stick doesn't have any properties in W1, Plantinga would say. How is that? Plantinga distinguishes between a *de dicto* and a *de re* reading at W1. He will claim that, *de dicto*, the proposition *The standard metre stick, if it exists, is 1m long in* α is true in W1. But read *de re*, we have a falsehood in W1: *The standard metre stick has the property being 1m long in* α.

So, though I am sympathetic to Yagisawa's conclusion—that serious actualism is false—I don't think that the serious actualist has any reason to accept (R), Yagisawa's main principle in his argument.

2.3.2 Arguments by Example

I think the most compelling arguments for the independence thesis are those that point to particular examples where things have properties though they don't exist. Some examples of properties that Socrates might have at worlds where he doesn't exist include *nonexistence* (Pollock 1984, 1985), *being self-identical*, *being identical with Socrates*, various negative properties like *not being a number* and *not being a mountain*, and *being referred to by "Socrates"* (Salmon 1987). Some examples of properties Socrates might have though he no longer exists (assuming presentism and ceasing to exist after bodily death) include *nonexistence, being self-identical, being identical with Socrates*, various negative properties like those mentioned above, and intentional properties like *being studied, being talked about, being appreciated*, and the like. In addition, singular propositions about Socrates may be possible at worlds and times where Socrates doesn't exist (Salmon 1987). In Section 2.4, we will discuss various proposals for the sorts of properties that objects may have when they don't exist. But the sorts of cases above are what philosophers who accept the independence thesis point to as counterexamples to serious actualism or serious presentism. I don't think there are knockdown arguments for any of them in the literature; rather, the philosopher is supposed to see the appeal of objects exemplifying some or all of these properties or standing in some or all of these relations though they don't exist.

2.4 Properties Had by Things That Don't Exist

There are various positions one might take as to the properties that objects that don't exist may have or not have. It's worth noting upfront that once one allows Socrates to have even something like *nonexistence* at worlds or times where he doesn't exist, one can no longer have any in-principle objection to objects that don't exist having properties. Socrates' having even *nonexistence* falsifies serious actualism or serious presentism all by itself. It opens the door to Socrates' having other properties beyond just *nonexistence*.

As we discuss properties that objects that don't exist have and don't have, it is worth considering other debates where people have wanted to say that objects have only some of the properties ordinary present and existing objects have. One area of debate where we see posits of objects lacking some of their ordinary properties is in the philosophy of time. A concern with a growing block view of time (on which the past and present exist, but the future doesn't) is skepticism about knowing what time is present. The eternalist takes "now" to be an indexical term, picking out something like the time of utterance within the larger spacetime manifold. The presentist takes it to pick out what exists, full stop. But *prima facie*, the growing block theorist has elements of both theories in her metaphysics. On the one hand, there is an edge of objective becoming. On the other hand, there are past utterances of "now." So what if the edge of objective becoming is sometime in the distant future? When I say "now it is 2022," and I take "now" to be picking out the present; I may be wrong. I may be picking out a time far in the past of the objective present.

Forrest (2004) replies to this sort of objection by denying that wholly past objects are conscious. So, I can deduce that I exist on the edge of temporal becoming because I know that I am conscious. And if I weren't, I of course wouldn't be wondering if I were on the leading edge of the growing block. So, when I note that now it is 2022, I know that 2022 is present. So, according to Forrest, past people exist, though they are not conscious now.

Another area in the philosophy of time where philosophers posit objects stripped of some of their properties is the moving spotlight view. The moving spotlighter thinks that past, present, and future are real. But she also believes in real temporal passage. She likens this passage to a spotlight moving across the entire spacetime manifold. This spotlight lights up the present. The moving spotlighter usually wants to say that present objects, by virtue of being present, have some metaphysical primacy over past and future objects. One way to make sense of this primacy is to strip past and future objects of some of their properties. In a recent book-length defense of the moving spotlight view, Ross Cameron says,

> It is a consequence of my view that Caesar exists now that he stands in a certain location relation now (and thereby is now a concrete individual), but that he now has no height, no mass, no ordinary 3D shape, etc. Indeed, the only properties Caesar has now are ones he always has (such as his temporal distributional property, his location to a certain region of spacetime, and his essential properties such as being concrete, being human, etc.), and his age, as well as the properties that follow from these. (Cameron 2015, p. 149)

So the past object, Caesar, lacks all sorts of properties that I, a present object, have. Indeed, Cameron strips his past objects of more properties than Forrest does. Forrest denies consciousness of Caesar. Cameron denies this too, as well as denying that he has all sorts of physical properties.

In areas outside the metaphysics of time, we also encounter people whose ontologies include objects that lack many properties one might have thought they had. Necessitists like Williamson (2013) and Linsky and Zalta (1994, 1996) claim that there are existing (though intuitively only possible) objects like Salmon (1987)'s Noman or my sister. Indeed, these objects, like all objects, exist in every world. How do we account for the fact that I say that I have no sister, and Salmon claims Noman doesn't exist? We say that in the actual world they aren't concrete. As a result, though, they lack all the ordinary properties that entail being concrete (having a body, for one).

Many Meinongians also tend to think that there are objects that lack a range of properties. Earlier Meinongians like Parsons (1980) or Routley (2018) think that there are incomplete objects that have only the properties that are used to characterize them. Some more recent Meinongians like Priest (2005, 2016) are stingier with the properties that nonexistent objects have. Priest says, in a symposium on Priest (2005)

> I take non-existent objects to have very few properties at the actual world. They can have intentional properties, such as being thought of, and logical properties, like being identical to or different from something. Crucially, they cannot have any property that entails that they enter into causal relations; for this would entail that they exist. (Priest 2008, p. 208)

Another Meinongian, Tim Crane, also is restrictive in properties that he allows nonexistent objects to have. In Crane (2013) he says,

> But despite its similarity to this important truth, Routley's claim [that Pegasus is a horse and Cerberus a dog] just quoted is actually false. Take his remark that Pegasus is a horse. Is Pegasus a horse in the same sense that the Darley Arabian is a horse? Routley will say yes ... But here are a few things we actually know about horses: they are normally born from other horses, as a result of mating between a male and female horse. No such thing happened to Pegasus: no act of mating resulted in the birth of Pegasus. They normally have four legs and the typical internal organs of mammals. Does Pegasus have such features? Routley may say: well, Pegasus does or it doesn't, depending on the characterization ... But surely if Pegasus really is a horse, in the sense that the Darley Arabian is a horse, then surely Pegasus must have many or all of the features of a horse. Otherwise what sense can we make of saying that it is a horse? But whether or not it has these features depends on what it is to be a horse, not on what characterization we choose. (p. 62)

He continues,

> Objects have natures. What their natures are is a matter of empirical or metaphysical study. But having some of these natures requires that those objects exist. It is in the nature of horses, planets, golden things, living things

(and so on) to exist. Non-existent things do not have what it takes to have the properties of these things. Non-existent objects cannot have properties like being a horse, being golden, being a detective, and nor can they stand in relations like killing. (Crane 2013, p. 63)

Which properties do nonexistent object have, then? Crane says that they have almost entirely *pleonastic* properties (the term comes from Schiffer 2003). These are properties that are dependent on our representing the object in some sort of way.

> Almost all of the pleonastic properties of non-existents are what Colin McGinn ... has called "representation-dependent" properties (McGinn 2000). That is, they are properties which depend upon the fact that the object is being represented in some way: in thought, language, pictures, and so on. Being a mythical horse is such a property, since something's being a mythical horse depends on there being a myth in which it is represented as a horse. Similarly, being a fictional detective is a representation-dependent property, since it depends on there being a fiction in which something is represented as a detective ... All properties of non-existents are representation-dependent, with the exception of the property of non-existence itself. (Crane 2013, p. 68)

So the only non-pleonastic properties that nonexistent objects have is *nonexistence*. All other properties they have are representation-dependent. (We will consider further the question of properties of nonexistent objects for the Meinongian in Chapter 7.)

We then have various debates in contemporary metaphysics where philosophers deny that some objects lack some or many of the properties that ordinary existing objects have. The independence actualist may well offer another case of this sort.

With these various examples in mind, I want to set out four different grades of independence actualism. There are possible positions between the four, so I don't intend the list to be exhaustive. But it will be useful in thinking about different positions an independence actualist might take.

1. **Minimalist Independence Actualism**: Objects that don't exist have only *nonexistence*.
2. **Sparse Independence Actualism**: Objects that don't exist have *nonexistence*, logical properties and relations (including *being*

self-identical, being referred to by N [where "N" is a name of them], and perhaps exemplifying their haecceity), and entailments of the logical properties and relations.
3. **Moderate Independence Actualism**: Objects that don't exist have some nonlogical properties and stand in some nonlogical relations. A view on which an object has its essential properties, its logical properties, and some "ordinary" properties—for example, *being a detective* or *wearing a deerstalker hat*—would be a moderate view.
4. **Maximalist Independence Actualism**: Objects that don't exist have all of their properties, save *existence*. Consider a world W where Socrates doesn't exist. Intuitively, Socrates has all the properties and stands in all the same relations at that world that an actualist would say he has (were that world actual), apart from *existence*.

Which of the four views should we adopt, assuming we find actualism and the independence thesis compelling? Many of the objections to objects' possessing particular properties though they don't exist are objections to their possessing any properties at all when they don't exist. We are beyond that objection with any of these views. One important consideration in choosing a particular sort of independence actualism centers on the amount of philosophical work each can do. Of course, if one thinks they have a serious argument against one of the more-rich sorts of independence actualisms, that will tell against adopting that sort of view. But in the decision calculus should be the amount each view can explain and the philosophical data it can account for. I say this in part because very rarely are there knockdown arguments in philosophy, much less in abstract metaphysics. One always has to decide whether an argument against a view is so serious as to override its theoretical virtues.

My claim then is this: We should adopt the independence actualist view that is strong enough to solve the philosophical problems we're trying to solve.

I anticipate an objection: But what if the objects that don't exist don't have the requisite properties or stand in the requisite relations to offer solutions to the philosophical problems in question? To give an answer to this objection, it is worth looking at the way David Lewis (1986) conceives of what warrants the acceptance of his modal concretist view. Lewis thinks that his metaphysics of concrete possible worlds and individuals in those worlds does a great deal of philosophical work. He also thinks that he can address objections to his metaphysics. If a view does a great deal of work and isn't subject to serious objections, doesn't one then have good reason to accept it? He says,

> Why believe in a plurality of worlds?—Because the hypothesis is serviceable, and that is a reason to think that it is true. The familiar analysis of necessity as truth at all possible worlds was only the beginning. In the last two decades, philosophers have offered a great many more analyses that make reference to possible worlds, or to possible individuals that inhabit possible worlds. I find that record most impressive. (Lewis 1986, p. 3)

> If we want the theoretical benefits that talk of [concrete] possibilia brings, the most straightforward way to gain honest title to them is to accept such talk as the literal truth ... The benefits are worth their ontological cost. Modal realism is fruitful; that gives us good reason to believe it is true. Good reason; I do not say it is conclusive. Maybe the theoretical benefits to be gained are illusory, because the analyses that use [concrete] possibilia do not succeed on their own terms. Maybe the price is higher than it seems because [Lewis' concretist metaphysics] has unacceptable hidden implications. (Lewis 1986, p. 4)

Lewis's claim (as evidenced particularly from the totality of his work) is that the utility of his metaphysics gives *prima facie* reason to think that it is true. When we add forceful replies to objections to the metaphysics, one has good reason to accept the view. Lewis sets out to do both of these in the course of Lewis (1986). Now, I think that Lewis is wrong here on both counts: That it does the explanatory work he says it does, and that it is free from objections. But we can learn something from Lewis's overall strategy. I have argued in this chapter that none of the arguments that would tell against independence actualism are cogent. I will argue in the rest of the book—particularly in the next chapter—that independence actualism is useful for solving a variety of philosophical problems. The conjunction of these two facts constitutes a good case for accepting independence actualism.

Back to the objection: What if the objects that don't exist don't have the right properties or stand in the right relations? Imagine a parallel objection to Lewis: What if the concrete possible worlds didn't have the right individuals standing in the right relations to get our claims about modality, properties, intentionality, or propositions right? What if every other concrete possible world contained only a single coffee cup?[10] Then the view wouldn't do any work. We can see then that the work a view like Lewis's can do depends on how the concrete possible worlds and individuals are.

Lewis would rightly reply that he is justified in positing that there are possible worlds and possible individuals of the right sort to do the explanatory work he wants his view to do. I mean, that's the view, and its explanatory power gives reason to accept it, absent strong reasons against it.

In this, we take an approach similar to that of some Meinongians (e.g., Jacquette 2015; Parsons 1980; Routley 2018) who adopt some sort of comprehension or characterization principle that guides her positing of nonexistent objects. For instance, Parsons adopts the principle

> (2) For any set of nuclear properties, some object has all the properties in that set and no other nuclear properties. (1980, p. 19)

There are perhaps two ways of taking this sort of principle. Sometimes, characterization principles have a whiff of anti-realism about them; there comes to be in the scope of our widest quantifiers a nonexistent object that has the properties in question as a result of our entertaining the nuclear properties in question. But I don't think this is what contemporary Meinongians mean to say, or at least what they *ought* to say about characterization principles. A better way to understand a principle like Parsons's (2) is that the nonexistent objects are *already there*, and our contemplating the nuclear properties in question is a sort of reference-fixing device. But then we might ask, what if there *isn't*, after all, a nonexistent object that has the properties in question? How can you be certain that there is the requisite nonexistent object with the right properties? If there's not, how do you account for the particular case of intentionality or fictional discourse or the like?

I think the Meinongian would be within her rights to claim that there is a nonexistent object with the requisite properties is a posit of her theory, and she is *prima facie* entitled to her theory's posits. This strikes me as a perfectly appropriate response to this concern. After all, it is Parsons's theory that there are the requisite nonexistent objects to account for phenomena of intentionality, fiction, and the like.

I think of independence actualism the same way. We are justified in adopting an independence actualism on which objects that don't exist exemplify the properties and stand in the relations needed to do the explanatory work we want to have done. We are warranted in this so long as there are not strong objections to that sort of independence actualism. I have argued and will argue further that there aren't.

In Chapter 3 we will look at how different independence actualisms may reply to a wide range of philosophical problems. We then will be in a position to reflect on which grade of independence actualism we ought to adopt.

3

The Utility of Independence Actualism

In this chapter I want to set out a number of problems in contemporary metaphysics, philosophy of language, and philosophy of religion. We will look both at some of the standard replies to the problems and what the independence actualist might say about them. I will argue that the right sort of independence actualism constitutes a plausible response to each problem. In addition to giving motivation for accepting independence actualism, this will help us to get clear on the sort of properties we should think of objects' having and relations that they stand in at times and worlds where they don't exist.

3.1 Presentism: Grounding Past Truths

Grounding worries arise naturally for the presentist-actualist. Here, I want to consider two sorts of grounding problems: grounding past truths and grounding cross-time relations. We tackle these in order.

Presentism is the view that whatever exists (read the quantifier here as widely as possible) is present. Equivalently, presentism is the view that there are no wholly past or future entities. The presentist-actualist has a *prima facie* problem of accounting for the truth of propositions about the past. For instance, the proposition

(P1) <World War I occurred before World War II.>

is true. But what makes it true, if neither war exists on account of being a wholly past object?[1] There are various things that a presentist might say when asked for a truthmaker for (P1) (see Caplan and Sanson 2010 and Davidson 2013 for an overview of the problem and solutions). Here are a few.

In response to these sorts of grounding concerns, presentists have looked to things that exist now or properties that are instantiated now to do the required grounding. One strategy that presentists have adopted has come to be called "Lucretianism" (see Bigelow 1996). Lucretianism is the view that the universe has the right past-directed properties to ground truths about the past. In the case of (P1), the universe has the property *being such that the First World War occurred before the Second World War*. Often, people will object to this sort of solution as cheating (Sider 2001). One may ask the Lucretian why the universe has this past-directed property if presentism is true. What makes it the case that the universe has the property *being such that the First World War occurred before the Second World War*? This property instantiation seems brute and *ad hoc*, and the Lucretian fix seems unsatisfying.

Another strategy that presentists have adopted is to ground past truths in divine cognition (Rhoda 2009). On this view, the reason (P1) is true is because God believes it is true. God's mind acts as a sort of recording device, and this will provide a ground for past truths. Of course, this solution isn't available to a nontheist. Furthermore, there is still something ungrounded here: We should want to know why God's belief that (P1) is true. What makes it true?

A third solution to concerns about grounding past truths is to allow abstract times to do the grounding (Crisp 2007). On this view, times are abstract objects in the way that possible worlds are abstract objects for most actualists. Intuitively, they are something like maximal states of affairs that do, will, or did obtain. There is some sort of primitive ordering relation on them that organizes them in the right fashion (Crisp 2007 uses the *being earlier than* relation). We have a definition of existence at a time that is analogous to existing at a world (something like, if that time were present, the thing would exist). Then what makes (P1) true is that the abstract time at which the First World War exists is earlier than the abstract time at which the Second World War exists.

I think this is quite a nice solution for the presentist (I defend it in Davidson 2013). But it still has an ungrounded element in it—the primitive ordering relation on the abstract times. It would be nice if the presentist could avoid that sort of thing.

A final thing that the presentist has said in reply to these sorts of grounding worries is to reject the need for grounding. Trenton Merricks (2007) is a presentist who thinks that truths about the past are simply ungrounded, and there is nothing wrong with this fact. He rejects the various general grounding principles that generate the concerns about truthmakers for past truths.

That said, it would be nice if the presentist could point to a ground for past truths and could point to a ground that doesn't build in primitive features that will draw accusations of cheating from non-presentists. This of course is consistent with thinking that if the presentist can't, so much the worse for the general grounding demands that generate the grounding worries.

The presentist who is an independence actualist has a story to tell about how propositions like (P1) are made true. To see what a presentist-independence actualist would have to say about the truth of (P1), it is worthwhile to consider how the eternalist—who thinks past, present, and future are equally real—would ground the truth of (P1). The eternalist believes that the events the First World War and the Second World War exist (where our quantifiers are read in an unrestricted fashion) and that the First World War occurs earlier than the Second World War in the spacetime order. Thus, for the eternalist, (i) the First World War and the Second World War exist, and (ii) the First World War stands in the *being earlier than* relation to the Second World War. These explain what makes (P1) true.

The presentist who is an independence actualist can model her explanation for the truth of (P1) on the eternalist's. She, of course, cannot say that the (concrete) events the First World War and the Second World War exist. But she can say that the First World War stands in the *being earlier than* relation to the Second World War. She may say this in spite of the fact that neither exists.

On this solution, there is no more "cheating" than there is on the eternalist's solution. In particular, there aren't primitive past-directed properties à la Lucretianism, nor are there abstract times with an unanalyzed ordering relation on them. The independence actualist has no need to adopt theism, much less a theism with ungrounded divine past-looking mental states. So this solution to grounding problems should appeal to those who are sympathetic to Sideresque criticisms of cheating with other standard replies to these problems, yet who wish to remain actualist-presentists.

I imagine a retort: This is all fine for (P1), which involves wholly past objects. What about grounding past properties of present objects? Consider

(P2) <Obama was a child.>

We aren't able to appeal to past objects' having properties and standing in relations to account for the truth of (P2), it would seem. We are concerned, rather, with properties of presently existing Obama. Isn't the presentist committed to a cheating-type solution here?

Perhaps. Suppose that the independence actualist-presentist weren't able to solve all grounding problems by allowing objects that don't exist to exemplify properties and stand in relations. It's still important that she can solve grounding problems that are about wholly past entities.

However, with the right metaphysics the presentist might appeal to past objects' having properties and standing in relations to account for the truth of propositions like (P2). Suppose that Obama has instantaneous temporal parts, perhaps that coincide with an enduring entity. Then we can account for the truth of (P2) by appealing to past Obama temporal parts: (P2) is true because a past temporal part of Obama has the property *being a child*. If one is a presentist and feels the bite of grounding concerns, one then could adopt a presentist-perdurantist ontology to avoid these concerns.

It is worth noting that the presentist-independence actualist who addresses grounding problems in this manner isn't thereby a Meinongian. There are no nonexistent entities in the scope of our widest quantifiers on this solution. In particular, the First World War and the Second World War are not nonexistent entities in the account. But they *do* stand in temporal relations to each other, and their standing in the right temporal relations suffices for the truth of (P1).[2]

3.2 Presentism: Cross-Time Relations

The presentist-actualist faces a different challenge similar to that of grounding past truths. That is grounding cross-time relations. The problem of cross-time relations is a well-known difficulty for presentists (see Crisp 2005; Davidson 2003b, for discussion). The explosion at the nuclear power plant a few seconds ago caused the breaking of the windows now. I am of the same nationality as Abraham Lincoln. These and similar claims seem to involve relations holding between wholly past (let us so stipulate in the Lincoln case) individuals and present ones. But how can that be if presentism is true, and there are no objects that don't exist?

This is a difficult problem for the presentist, and presentists have given a number of different replies. Some presentists have said that sentences that certainly appear to involve relations holding between present and non-present objects actually involve relations between presently existing things. So rather than my standing in a relation to Abraham Lincoln, perhaps I stand in a relation to properties or states of affairs that always exist. (But, of course, it sure *seems* that I stand in relations to past individuals who don't exist now.) Others have denied the truth of claims like my being of the same nationality as Lincoln, or that past things cause present things. (But, many of these cross-time relational propositions look to be *true*.) Still others have denied that the truth of a sentence like "I am of the same nationality as Abraham Lincoln" involves a relation holding at all; perhaps, rather, it involves only my having a certain relational property. (But, how can the relational property hold without the corresponding relation also holding?)

However, the most straightforward path out of these problems for the actualist-presentist is simply to be an independence actualist. Consider again how the eternalist would explain the truth of cross-time relational sentences like those mentioned earlier. The explosion at the power plant doesn't exist now, but it does exist. So it can stand in causal relations with the breaking of the window now. Abraham Lincoln doesn't exist now, but he does exist. So he can stand in nationality relations with me. The presentist by adopting independence actualism can ground the truth of cross-time causal relations in an analogous sort of way. The event of the explosion at the power plant doesn't exist, but it can stand in causal relations to the present breaking of the window. Lincoln doesn't exist, but he can stand in nationality relations with me; and so on. For the presentist who is an independence actualist, the explanation of the truth of sentences involving cross-time relations doesn't involve the sorts of contortions one sees in the extant presentist literature.[3]

Accepting independence actualism then allows the presentist-actualist to reply to two of the most serious problems for an actualist presentism: grounding past truths and cross-time relations. We should note that these sorts of solutions push the independence actualist in the direction of a view on which objects that don't exist have an abundance of properties. The past explosion at the nuclear plant has to be powerful for it to cause the window to break. Lincoln must have a nationality for me to stand in the *same nationality* relation to him. It looks like we're headed in the direction of one of the richer sorts of independence actualism, at least if we want to address presentist concerns with cross-time relations with it. We will return to this at the end of the chapter.

3.3 Direct Reference and Empty Terms

Grounding or truthmaking worries arise for those who believe in singular propositions with concrete contingent individuals as constituents. I want to consider here problems that arise from empty terms. In Chapter 6 we will consider at length the view that Plantinga (1979, 1983) calls "existentialism"— that singular propositions and haecceities are dependent for their existence on the things they are "about."

Belief in Russellian singular propositions that have referents of rigid singular terms as constituents is widespread (see, e.g., Kaplan 2007a, 2007b; Salmon 1986). The view that the semantic contents of rigid terms are the referents of these terms has come to be known as *direct reference*. There is an immediate problem that arises for the direct reference theorist—empty terms.

Suppose that direct reference is true. Here is an example to help illustrate the problem of empty terms for the direct reference theorist. Suppose that I come to exist as the result of in vitro fertilization. As a teenager I am shown a frozen early-stage blastocyst from the same batch I am from. I am told that it will be implanted, and thus I will have a sibling. (I am happy about this, as [suppose] I am an only child.) For legal reasons, I am not able to meet my sibling until she (or he) turns 18, however. In subsequent years, in the absence of knowing her (or his) name, I decide to call my sibling "Sib."[4] I then believe that the sentence

(S1) Sib is my sibling

expresses a true proposition, as I believe that the blastocyst was implanted and has given rise to a human being. I assert (S1) in conversations with other people when I talk about the fact that I actually have a sibling. Suppose also that I am on good terms with God, and God has promised to answer one question I ask. So I ask God just after I've seen the blastocyst, "What would a person who came from a blastocyst like the one I saw be like?" God gives me a very thorough description: "A person coming from that blastocyst would be female, medium-height, prone to skin cancer, likely to live to an old age," and so on. The description goes on for some time. Thus, in the case of Sib, I have a rich description of what this individual would be like. She'd come from a particular blastocyst and would exhibit a wide range of qualities—many of which God has told me about.

Suppose, further, though, that the information I was given about the blastocyst's being implanted was false. The blastocyst wasn't implanted. Rather, it was destroyed shortly after I saw it. So "Sib" doesn't actually refer to anyone. So (S1) doesn't express a complete proposition for the direct reference theorist. Yet, I asserted it meaningfully when I earlier believed that I had a sibling. How could this be if (S1) doesn't express a complete proposition?

There are various things that direct reference theorists have had to say at this point. Often, they appeal to gappy or partial propositions to account for semantic and psychological phenomena around sentences like (S1). Compare (S1) to another sentence where there are no empty terms:

(S2) Mark is my sibling.

We can represent the proposition that (S2) expresses as:

(P2) <**Mark**, *being my sibling*>.[5]

(P2) has parts, or something like parts. In the "subject" part is Mark. In the "predicate" part is the property *being my sibling*. If we return to (S1), we see that we can represent the proposition (or partial proposition) expressed by (S1) as

(P1) < _, *being my sibling*>.

(P1) looks like (P2), save for the fact that (P1) has a gap in it where (P2) has Mark.

Some direct reference theorists appeal to entities like (P1) to explain the appearance of sentences like (S1) being meaningful and expressing propositions. (S1) *almost* or *sort of* expresses a complete proposition. There are different things that direct reference theorists have wanted to say at this point, though. Perhaps the person best known for the gappy or partial propositions strategy is David Braun (1993, 2005).[6] Braun gives an account on which sentences with empty rigid terms may be counted as true. He says,

> We can state truth conditions for simple atomic propositions ... to cover unfilled propositions. If P is a proposition having a single subject position and a one-place property position, then P is true iff the subject position is filled by one, and only one, object, and it exemplifies the property filling the property position. If P is not true, then it is false. (Braun 1993, p. 463)

Furthermore, on Braun's account, there is one proposition expressed by all true negative existential sentences:

(N) < <_, existence>, NEG>[7]

We see that the first part of the proposition, the gappy proposition <_, existence>, is false by the aforementioned criterion. So the negation of it is true.

Why are we inclined to think that different negative existential sentences express different propositions? Braun claims this is as a result of having different belief states from encountering (N) through the lens of different sentences.

Braun is not alone in positing an alternative semantics to account for the truth of negative existential sentences. Keith Donnellan (1974, p. 25) says,

> I will suggest a rule, using the notion of a block, that purports to give the truth conditions for negative existence statements containing a name ... [T]he rule can be expressed as follows:
>
> (R) If N is a proper name that has been used in predicative statements with the intention to refer to some individual, then ⌜N does not exist⌝ is true if and only if the history of those uses ends in a block.

Nathan Salmon (1998) also appeals to gappy propositions as a way to address problems with empty rigid terms. His account is similar to that of Braun's, though he denies that atomic gappy propositions have truth values. Again, like Braun, negative existentials come out sometimes true when the negation is read as applying to the entire proposition. So I may utter "Sib does not exist," and when we read the negation as applying to the gappy proposition <_, existence>, we get a truth.

There are a number of philosophers who appeal to pragmatic considerations in explaining our intuitions around empty rigid terms (e.g., Adams, Fuller, and Stecker 1997; Adams and Stecker 1994; Soames 2002; Taylor 2000). These philosophers explain that we sometimes take gappy propositions to be true with the fact that the sentences expressing these propositions pragmatically implicate other, complete propositions. We mistake the implicated propositions for the semantic contents of the sentences with empty terms.

Other philosophers have given up direct reference and have taken the semantic contents of rigid terms to be individual essences (things like haecceities or world-indexed properties) of the referents of the terms (e.g., Plantinga 1974, 1978). On this strategy, one can model talk of Russellian singular propositions by using necessarily existing properties to "go proxy" for contingently existing individuals that would be propositional constituents.

Another sort of route that the direct reference theorist may take with respect to empty rigid terms is to claim that, appearances notwithstanding, they aren't actually empty. A way to do this in a manner consistent with actualism is to adopt necessitism (Linsky and Zalta 1994, 1996; Williamson 2013). So when I utter (S1), "Sib" *does* refer. It just doesn't refer to a concrete entity; but rather to a non-abstract, contingently non-concrete entity. Or, of course, the direct reference theorist may adopt a Meinongian position on which the gap in a proposition is filled with a nonexistent entity.[8]

Independence actualism offers another way for the direct reference theorist to account for the meaningfulness and truth of sentences with empty (or apparently empty) rigid terms, such as with (S1). In particular, there are two moves the independence actualist may make. First, she can say that "Sib" in (S1) *does* refer, even though its referent does not exist. That is, "Sib" may stand in the *referring* relation to Sib, even though there is no Sib. Second (and this is my preferred strategy), the independence actualist may account for the meaningfulness of (S1) by allowing it to express a complete proposition, even though Sib doesn't exist. That is, Sib may be a constituent of the proposition expressed by (S1) in spite of the fact that there is no Sib.

To see what we're after in this second strategy, consider the sentence

(S3) Michelle Obama lives in Chicago.

The direct reference theorist will claim that the proposition this sentence expresses has Michelle Obama as a constituent. We may ask of this proposition, why does it have Michelle Obama as a constituent rather than, say, Michelle Yeoh? It is because Michelle Obama stands in the right sorts of propositional formation relations (both qualitative and quidditative) to the other elements of the proposition, and Michelle Yeoh doesn't. The problem the actualist direct reference theorist appears to have with the proposition expressed by (S1) is that Sib doesn't exist and thus can't be related to the rest of the propositional elements putatively expressed by (S1). But if we accept that objects may exemplify properties and stand in relations even when they don't exist, this goes away. We can maintain that Sib can stand in the requisite propositional composition relations to the rest of the contents of the proposition expressed by (S1) so as to result in a complete singular proposition that is expressed.

The independence actualist may claim that the proposition expressed by

(S1) Sib is my sister

and the proposition expressed by

(S2) Mark is my sister

exist. Each sentence expresses a complete proposition. One of the constituents of the proposition expressed by (S1) doesn't exist. But it still stands in the right sort of relations to the other elements that make up the proposition for there to be a complete proposition expressed by (S1). Indeed, Sib stands in the same (qualitative) propositional composition relations with the proposition expressed by (S1) that Mark does with the proposition expressed by (S2).

Why think that the proposition expressed by (S1) has Sib as a constituent, even though there is no Sib? It seems to me entirely appropriate for the independence actualist to point to two commonly held (though often thought to be in some tension) features of propositions: Propositions exist necessarily, and they have their constituents essentially. They have their constituents essentially by standing in propositional composition relations to their constituents essentially (and necessarily).

This allows the direct reference theorist to avoid problems that arise with the other accounts of empty terms that we just considered. It allows one to avoid the (perhaps) troublesome metaphysics of gappy or incomplete propositions. It allows one to bypass completely the question of alternate truth conditions for gappy or incomplete propositions or for functions on them. With respect to the individual essence proxy route, if one thinks of haecceities as "thisnesses" in the way Adams (1979, 1981) does; one may be inclined to think that an haecceity exists only if the object that instantiates it does. Furthermore, one gives up a view on which the entirety of the semantic content of a rigid term is its referent if one accepts that the semantic content of rigid terms is an haecceity. This is a view close to direct reference, but it's not direct reference.[9] Using Plantinga-style world-indexed properties (Plantinga 1978) will almost certainly seem too Fregean for those attracted to direct reference semantics. With respect to the pragmatic implicature route, there are reasons to doubt that competent language speakers are ignorant of meaning in the way the pragmatic theorists mentioned above posit (Caplan 2007; Reimer 2001). Furthermore, the independence actualist is able to avoid necessitism with its necessarily existing contingently concrete objects and Meinongianism with its nonexistent objects. Thus, there are costs to these other sorts of views that the independence actualist may avoid.

We should also note that the independence actualist has a compelling account of the truth of negative existentials as well. Consider the following sentence:

(S4) Sib does not exist.

The independence actualist faces no temptation to embrace gappy propositions in giving an account of the proposition expressed by (S4). Sib, though she doesn't exist, may stand in the requisite propositional composition relations such that there is a complete proposition expressed by (S4). Furthermore, Sib can exemplify *nonexistence*, even though Sib does not exist.

It may be the case that singular propositions about individuals who don't exist are often difficult for us to grasp and talk about. The Sib case is designed to let us pick out an individual singular proposition in ways that we wouldn't otherwise be able to. But the fact that we can't grasp or refer to many singular propositions about nonexistent objects doesn't say anything about whether they exist. It just says that we have cognitive and epistemic limitations that prevent us from entertaining them. The independence actualist may insist that the singular propositions exist at every world, whether or not the object they are about exists at that world.

3.4 Molinism and Counterfactuals of Freedom

Various concerns around grounding God's knowledge arise for the theist. I want to consider two in this chapter: grounding problems from Molinism and grounding problems from divine foreknowledge. In this section we will consider those of Molinism.

Medieval Christian philosophers divided God's knowledge into two sorts. On the one hand, there was God's *natural knowledge*. God's natural knowledge was of necessary truths, and God had it logically prior to the decision to make a particular world actual (or "prevolitionally"). So, prior to deciding to make the actual world, α, actual, God knew that *2+2=4* and *Socrates isn't possibly a sandwich*.[10] On the other hand, there was God's *free knowledge*. God's free knowledge was of contingent truths, and God had it after deciding to make a particular world actual (postvolitionally). So only after deciding to make α actual does God know *the summit of Mt. Everest is the tallest physical feature on earth in 2025*.

Luis de Molina, a sixteenth-century Spanish philosopher, argued that there was a third sort of knowledge situated conceptually between God's free knowledge and natural knowledge. Molina called it *middle knowledge*. God's middle knowledge is like God's natural knowledge in that it is prior to the decision to make a particular world actual. It also is like God's free knowledge in that the propositions known *via* God's middle knowledge are contingent. With his middle knowledge, God knows *counterfactuals of freedom*—counterfactual propositions with properties about libertarian-free actions in their consequents. Thus, with his middle knowledge, God knows prior to actualizing any world that (say) if I were offered an iced coffee in my present circumstances, I would accept it. If God has middle knowledge, God has significant control over the way things turn out in any world he actualizes—even if there are libertarian-free creatures in it. God knows which circumstances will produce particular libertarian-free actions prior to actualizing a world, and God simply can actualize those circumstances so as to bring about those libertarian-free actions he wishes.

There is a puzzle, however, in recent times that was first spotted by Robert Adams (1977). What makes these contingently true counterfactual propositions true prior to God's actualizing a world?[11] The Molinist could try to say that God makes these counterfactuals of freedom true. But that would seem to rule out libertarian free will that involves being able to do otherwise. The Molinist could say that these propositions are true but ungrounded—not made true by anything. But this seems undesirable if it can be avoided. What the Molinist ought to say, it would seem, is that counterfactuals of freedom are made true by the individuals the propositions are about. What makes it true that I would accept an iced coffee if I were offered it in my present circumstances are facts about *me*. But the Molinist thinks that counterfactuals of freedom are true logically prior to any world's being actual and thus logically prior to my existing. It is thus difficult, if actualism is true, to see how facts about me could make counterfactuals of freedom true when they are true. These sorts of concerns about grounding have been seen to be the principal objection to Molinism (Hasker 1989). The standard Molinist reply to these grounding worries is to deny that counterfactuals of freedom need grounding (Flint 1998; Merricks 2007; Plantinga 1985a). It would be better for the Molinist, of course, if the Molinist could find some way to tell a story on which it is facts about me that make counterfactuals of freedom about me true. People who ask for grounds for truths in cases like those of counterfactuals of freedom are not likely to be satisfied with the retort that their initial demand was somehow illegitimate. But I think there actually is a different sort of reply that the actualist-Molinist can give at this point; this involves accepting independence actualism. The independence actualist can maintain that I make counterfactuals of freedom about me true. In fact, I can do this even prior to God's actualizing a world. How precisely does this go? Consider the grounding relation (such as it is—more on this in the next paragraph) that I stand in to counterfactuals of freedom when I exist. (I have in mind here just the relation that holds between facts about a libertarian-free action and the person who performs that action. Also, we may note that the libertarian may think that there are counterfactuals of freedom true about me now, whether or not any were true before actualizing a world.) Call that relation "R." The actualist-Molinist who is an independence actualist then can hold that R may hold even logically prior to God's actualizing a world.

This solution may not solve all related Molinist grounding worries, for grounding problems may arise even for someone who thinks that there are counterfactuals of freedom that are true only after a world is actualized.

Suppose now it is true of me that *if I were offered a cup of coffee, I would freely accept it*. This is a contingently true proposition; there are worlds where it is false. What makes it the case that it is true rather than false? Facts about me can't entail its truth; these are counterfactuals involving libertarian freedom. Thus, there still may be seen to be something ungrounded here, as there is for any libertarian view.

But the independence actualist has an answer to the particular grounding problems that arise specifically from prevolitionally true counterfactuals of freedom. There is no more a problem grounding their truth than there is grounding the truth of postvolitionally true counterfactuals of freedom.

As before, we can say all of this and not have to give up being card-carrying actualists. On this picture, I am not a nonexistent object prior to God's actualizing a world. But in adopting independence actualism, I can stand in grounding relations prior to God's actualizing a world, and standing in those relations is sufficient for the counterfactual of freedom's being true.

3.5 Divine Foreknowledge

A grounding problem not dissimilar to that had by Molinists arises for those who think that God has foreknowledge of libertarian-free actions. We might think of it as a special case of grounding worries having to do with cross-time relations, but it usually is treated as a *sui generis* sort of grounding problem. The problem can be put as follows. Suppose we want to say that God knows that in 10 minutes I will take a drink of coffee. What grounds God's knowledge in this case? In particular, what makes it true that in 10 minutes I will drink coffee, such that God can know this proposition? We would like to say it has to do with the concrete event of my drinking coffee, in 10 minutes. But suppose that because some non-eternalist theory of time (like presentism) is true, that event won't exist (or won't have the relevant properties to do grounding work) for 10 minutes. What makes the proposition true *now* that I drink coffee *then*?

There have been a variety of types of replies to this concern. Some theists have maintained foreknowledge of future libertarian-free actions by embracing eternalism. These philosophers maintain that the concrete event of my drinking coffee in 10 minutes does, in fact, exist. Other theists have denied that God has foreknowledge of future libertarian-free actions (Hasker 1989). Yet others have appealed to irreducibly future-directed states of affairs or propositions or properties (compare to strategies like Lucretianism with grounding in presentist contexts).

All these solutions have costs. But there is another solution that the actualist-theist could avail herself of—that involves accepting independence actualism. If one accepts the independence thesis, then one is able to maintain that it is the concrete event of my drinking coffee in 10 minutes that makes it the case that God knows now that in 10 minutes I will drink coffee. To see how this would go; consider the grounding relation that would hold between God's present belief that in 10 minutes I will drink coffee and the concrete event of my drinking coffee in 10 minutes, if eternalism were true. Call that relation "R." If one accepts the independence thesis, one can maintain that R holds even if the event of my drinking coffee doesn't exist. So God can have foreknowledge of my future actions. Thus, there are the resources for the actualist-theist to reply to grounding worries about foreknowledge without adopting any of the standard sorts of solutions noted above.

3.6 Rigid Designation

Nathan Salmon gives two ways that a term might be rigid.

> Perhaps the most frequently intended notion of a rigid designator is that of an expression which designates the same thing with respect to every possible world in which that thing exists, and which designates nothing with respect to possible worlds in which that thing does not exist ... [L]et us say that such expressions are *persistently rigid designators* ...
>
> Another sort of rigid designator is an expression which designates the same thing with respect to every possible world, period. Let us call expressions of this sort *obstinately rigid designators*. (Salmon 1981, pp. 33–4; emphasis in original)

Prima facie, there is a problem with the concept of obstinately rigid terms, at least in some cases. How can a term, say the name "Michelle Obama," refer to Michelle Obama in worlds where she doesn't exist? How can a term that denotes a contingently existing object be obstinately rigid?

To see what the independence actualist has to say about this, let us first consider what it is for a name to refer to a bearer. A name refers to a bearer just if the name bears the *referring* relation to the bearer. Now, there are various accounts of the particular relations that need to hold between name and bearer for the *referring* relation to obtain; I will eschew those debates here. Once we see that referring consists in a relation holding between name and bearer (however that relation comes to hold), we can see that the independence actualist may hold that this relation obtains between name and bearer even in worlds where the bearer doesn't exist.

Some people think that it is important that rigid terms be thought of as obstinately rigid (Kaplan 2007b; Salmon 1981). It's not my purpose here to evaluate these arguments (see Murday 2013 for discussion of some of them). But if one thought that the concept of obstinate rigidity for designators of contingent objects was problematic *per se*, the independence actualist has a story to tell on which obstinate rigidity in these cases makes sense.

3.7 Actualist Modal Truth Conditions

Another reason for accepting the independence thesis is its utility in giving actualist truth conditions for modal discourse. In "Actualism and Possible Worlds," Alvin Plantinga uses haecceities to give actualist truth conditions to modal sentences. Consider the following sentence:

(S5) It is possible there exist an object that doesn't actually exist.

The Kripke-semantics for modal logic would suggest something like the following account of (S5)'s truth: There is an object x in the union of all objects actual and possible; x doesn't exist at α, though x does exist at another world W.

This presents a problem for the actualist: In giving an account of (S5)'s truth, we seem to commit ourselves to there being nonexistent objects. At α, we appeal to the union of all actual and possible objects and select a merely possible object from it. Plantinga gives alternate truth conditions for (S5): (S5) is true just if there is an haecceity that isn't exemplified at α but is exemplified at another world W.

People like Christopher Menzel (1990) and Allen McMichael (1983) have argued that Plantinga's theory isn't really an actualist theory. His unexemplified haecceities go proxy for nonexistent objects and aren't sufficiently different from nonexistent objects to class Plantinga's theory as an actualist theory. We will take up this debate further in Chapter 6. We may note here, however, that there is an alternate route to truth conditions for modal sentences available for the actualist. The independence actualist may say that an object x exemplifies *nonexistence* and *possibly existing* (or *nonexistence* and *existing in W*, where W≠α) at α. It may do so even though x is not in the scope of our widest quantifiers at α. This will yield the truth of (S5), and one may arrive at these truth conditions without Menzel–McMichael type objections that one isn't *really* an actualist because of the employment of unexemplified haecceities.

3.8 Lessons

In this chapter I have shown how the independence actualist may reply to a wide variety of problems in contemporary philosophy. (We will consider more in Chapter 4.) It's worth taking stock of where we are at this point. In Chapter 2, we looked at four grades of independence actualism:

1. **Minimalist Independence Actualism**: Objects that don't exist have only *nonexistence*.
2. **Sparse Independence Actualism**: Objects that don't exist have *nonexistence*, logical properties and relations (including *being self-identical*, *being referred to by N* [where "N" is a name of them], and perhaps exemplifying their haecceity), and entailments of the logical properties and relations.
3. **Moderate Independence Actualism**: Objects that don't exist have some nonlogical properties and stand in some nonlogical relations. A view on which an object has its essential properties, its logical properties, and some "ordinary" properties—for example, *being a detective* or *wearing a deerstalker hat*—would be a moderate view.
4. **Maximalist Independence Actualism**: Objects that don't exist have all of their properties, save *existence*. Consider a world W where Socrates doesn't exist. Intuitively, Socrates has all the properties and stands in all

the same relations at that world that an actualist would say he has (were that world actual), apart from *existence*.

I argued in Chapter 2 that we are justified in positing the grade of independence actualism we need to solve the philosophical problems we want to solve. We can see in the course of this chapter that objects that don't exist may exemplify a wide range of properties and stand in a wide range of relations, at least if the independence actualist (*qua* independence actualist) intends to solve the sorts of metaphysical and semantic problems we considered in this chapter. Thus, the sort of independence actualism we should adopt is at least Moderate Independence Actualism. So far as I can tell there is no *a priori* argument that commits us to something as strong as Maximalist Independence Actualism. So we will proceed in future chapters as though we have in mind a robust sort of Moderate Independence Actualism.

4

Actualism or Meinongianism?

Up to this point, I have defended the independence thesis. I have not said as much about the "actualism" part of independence actualism. A Meinongian also accepts the independence thesis; nonexistent objects can have properties and stand in relations for a Meinongian. Why, then, should we be actualists who accept the independence thesis, rather than Meinongians? My argument for actualism over Meinongianism is straightforward and comes in two parts. First, the independence actualist may account for the main phenomena that the Meinongian claims one needs nonexistent objects to account for. Second, the independence actualist's ontology has fewer, and fewer objectionable, entities than has the Meinongian's.

I want to consider here what I take to be the three main reasons typically given by Meinongians for accepting nonexistent objects: proper treatment of intentional verbs, negative existentials, and fictional discourse. I will set out why the Meinongian thinks that nonexistent objects are needed for accounting for data with each, and I will argue that the independence actualist may account for the same data with her metaphysics.

4.1 Intentional Verbs

The principal motivation for Meinongianism throughout its history has been its ability to give a uniform treatment of the semantics of intentional verbs, whether or not there exists an object that is the referent of the direct object of the verb. This was Meinong's (1960) main motivation for thinking there are objects beyond being, and it features centrally in the motivations for the theories of contemporary Meinongians like Rapaport (1978), Routley (2018,

p. 12), Parsons (1980, p. 32), Tomberlin and McGuinness (1994), Jacquette (2015, part one), Priest (2005, ch. 3), and Crane (2013, ch. 1).

Suppose it is true that Albertus Magnus searched for the Philosopher's Stone. (And suppose what he searched for was a stone rather than some mass substance.) Then we have some inclination to say the sentence

(S1) Albertus Magnus searched for the Philosopher's Stone

is true. Suppose also that just before beginning his search for the Philosopher's Stone, Magnus searched for his pen so that he could write of his endeavor to find the Philosopher's Stone. Then we have a strong inclination to say that

(S2) Albertus Magnus searched for his pen

is true. One way to explain the truth of (S2) is to say that the *searched for* relation held between Magnus and his pen. If we give the same sort of explanation to (S1), however, we run into trouble, for there doesn't seem to be anything Magnus is related to. How then do we make sense of the truth of (S1), if it is indeed true?

There are typically four sorts of solutions to this problem. The first is to adopt Meinongianism. On this solution we have Magnus in a relation to an object, the nonexistent object the Philosopher's Stone. In this way, the logical form of (S1) is the same as that of (S2) and in each case the sentence comes out true because of his relation to an object. With (S2), the *searched for* relation holds between Magnus and an existent object—his pen. With (S1), the *searched for* relation holds between Magnus and a nonexistent object—the Philosopher's Stone. That (S1) and (S2) have the same logical form on the Meinongian solution is thought to be a strength of it, as the two sentences have the same grammatical form.

A second solution is to claim that Albertus Magnus's search with (S1) involves a property: *being the Philosopher's Stone*, or *being a stone that turns lead into gold*, or the like. One variant of this has Magnus searching for the property itself (Chisholm 1986; Church 1956). Another variant has him looking for the instantiation of one of these sorts of properties. There are immediate objections that each version of this solution faces, though. One problem with the former is that what Albertus Magnus was searching for was a concrete object, rather than an abstract object. One problem with the latter is that it looks like it just redescribes our problem. The instantiation of these properties is something concrete, and in the case of (S1), we are back to wondering how Magnus could search for something concrete.

A third solution (or reply) is simply to deny the truth of (S1). The truth conditions for (S1) involve a relation, and one relatum of the relation is missing. We can tell a story about why one might be tempted to think that (S1) is true; perhaps Magnus says he's searching for some object, and acts like he is. But (S1) actually is false.

The fourth typical solution is to claim that (S1) has a different logical form than does (S2). The truth conditions for (S2) involve Magnus searching for an object—his pen. The truth conditions for (S1) involve something else; perhaps Magnus engaging in certain activities that are of the same type as others one engages in when looking for an ordinary existing object. If Albertus Magnus acts in this way, then we can say that (S1) comes out true. The problem here is that it threatens to make our natural language semantics *ad hoc* and piecemeal. It would be nice to be able to treat the logical forms of (S1) and (S2) as the same and give the same explanations of their truth in terms of Magnus's relation to an object. And it would be nice to do so without having Magnus searching for an abstract or nonexistent object.

It turns out that there is a way to do this, and that is to adopt independence actualism. The independence actualist can allow that Albertus Magnus stands in the *searching for* relation to the Philosopher's Stone, even though there is no Philosopher's Stone. Thus, (S1) may express a true proposition. This allows one to maintain that the logical forms of (S1) and (S2) are the same in the way the Meinongian can. But it doesn't commit one to having nonexistent objects in one's ontology.

There is a concern for the independence actualist: How does Albertus Magnus search *de re* for one particular object that doesn't exist—the Philosopher's Stone? Aren't there many such candidates that exemplify the requisite properties at the actual world? I think this is a serious concern, but isn't a problem for the independence actualist *per se*. Rather, it's a problem for accounts of the semantics of intentional verbs, more generally. It's certainly a problem for the Meinongian, for instance.[1] But there is a general question of what has to be true about a subject for claims like (S1) to come out true. The independence actualist could say various things about this. Maybe "The

Philosopher's Stone" should be taken to be vague, and we could supervaluate to give truth conditions for (S1). Maybe there aren't, after all, various, or various natural candidates for the reference of "The Philosopher's Stone." As a result, there is no problem of reference. Or perhaps there is a single-most natural candidate for the referent of "The Philosopher's Stone," and Albertus Magnus winds up searching for that as a result. Perhaps the Philosopher's Stone, though it doesn't exist, stands in causal relations, and Magnus is able to search for it that way. On this solution, one searches for it the way one searches for other long-lost artifacts, where a causal chain determines the object for which one searches. Or, maybe we want to say that (S1) isn't true unless Albertus Magnus has a rich-enough description (which may or may not involve causal relations) to pick out the Philosopher's Stone. There are, then, various things that the independence actualist might point to as mechanisms for dealing with these sorts of problems. The main point for us here is that there is a strategy for accounting for the truth of sentences with intentional verbs that doesn't involve searching for Meinongian objects or abstracta; that strategy involves adopting independence actualism.

Thus, on a main motivation for Meinongian theories, giving truth conditions for sentences with intentional verbs, we can see that the independence actualist fares as well as the Meinongian. But the independence actualist has a sparser ontology, and the objects eliminated (nonexistent objects) are objectionable to many on their own terms. I submit, then, that independence actualism is preferable to Meinongianism in giving an explanation of the semantics of intentional verbs.

4.2 Negative Existentials

A second motivation for Meinongianism is in giving truth conditions for negative existential sentences. If I say truly,

(S3) Anubis doesn't exist

a puzzle arises. Of what am I predicating nonexistence? If I'm predicating it of nothing, how is (S3) meaningful? Quine (1953) calls this puzzle "Plato's Beard." As we discussed in Chapter 3, there are various solutions to this puzzle.

The solution most important to us in this chapter is Meinongianism. The Meinongian can say that she is truly denying existence of the nonexistent object, Anubis, when she utters (S3). The ability of the Meinongian to explain the truth of sentences like (S3) is part of what motivated Russell's early Meinongianism in *The Principles of Mathematics* from 1903.[2]

The Meinongian has at least two strengths in her explanation of the truth of (S3). Both of these arise in the context of her ability to accept direct reference and avoid a description theory of rigid terms. This itself is a strength, for many think that the arguments in Kripke (1980) tell strongly against a description theory of rigid terms. First, she may avoid having the semantics of names change drastically in the context of existence statements (in the way they do in Donnellan 1974 and Braun 1993).[3] Second, the Meinongian is able to account for how (S3) expresses a complete proposition. The proposition expressed by (S3) will have a nonexistent object—Anubis—as part of it. But it will be complete.

The independence actualist, however, is able to give an account of the truth of (S3) that shares in these strengths. The independence actualist may accept direct reference and claim that "Anubis" in (S3) exhibits a semantics on a par with other names. In particular, there is no need for "blocks" (Donnellan 1974) or other such mechanisms to make a sentence like (S3) come out true. Second, the independence actualist may allow that (S3) expresses a complete proposition. Rather than the proposition expressed by (S3) having a nonexistent object in it (as the Meinongian would say), the independence actualist can say that Anubis is a constituent of the proposition expressed by (S3) even though Anubis doesn't exist. The independence actualist may say that Anubis stands in the requisite propositional compositional relations such that (S3) expresses a compete proposition.[4]

4.3 Fictional Discourse

A third primary motivation for Meinongian theories is their treatment of discourse involving fictional characters. As with intentional verbs, we see explicit appeal to true claims about fictional characters as data for Meinongian theories in many defenses of Meinongianism, for example, Routley (2018, ch.

1), Parsons (1980, ch. 2), Jacquette (1996, part 1), Jacquette (2015, chs. 13–14), Priest (2005, chs. 4, 6), and Crane (2013, ch. 3). There has been a great deal written about fictional characters in the past few decades, and I don't want to work through all of that here. What I do want to argue is that the Meinongian is not better off with respect to fictional characters than is the independence actualist.

The Meinongian has an advantage over those who think that fictional characters are actually existing abstract objects (Salmon 1998; Thomasson 1998; van Inwagen 1977).[5] If Sherlock Holmes is an abstract object, then it's false that Sherlock Holmes is a detective. Thus, those who think that fictional characters are abstracta typically invoke two different ways of a fictional character's relating to a property. Van Inwagen (1977) has it that Holmes *has* properties like *being a fictional character* and *being an abstract object* and *holds* properties like *being a detective* and *wearing a deerstalker hat*.

Many Meinongians have no need of this sort of distinction, at least when it comes to fictional characters. It will be true for classical Meinongians (what I will call "Robust Meinongians" in Chapter 7) like Meinong (1960), Parsons (1980), Routley (2018), and Jacquette (1996, 2015)—that full stop, that Sherlock Holmes is a detective, and that he exemplifies the property *wearing a deerstalker hat*. The view that fictional characters are abstract objects is supposed to allow for the truth of claims we make about fiction; for example, *Sherlock Holmes is a fictional character*, or (perhaps) *Sherlock Holmes was created by Arthur Conan Doyle*. But it can't allow for many important literal truths about the characters themselves. So the classical Meinongian has a *prima facie* advantage over the abstract object view of fictional characters in this respect.

The independence actualist can say everything important about fictional characters that the Meinongian can, save one: There are fictional characters in the scope of our widest quantifiers. It can be true at the actual world that Holmes is a detective, wears a deerstalker hat, and the like, even though Holmes doesn't exist at the actual world. How does Holmes get these properties at the actual world? Perhaps these properties are assigned to Holmes by authorial intention. If we take this route, it may go some way toward explaining the intuition that authors create fictional characters. Or perhaps the author of a story selects from many different individuals who don't exist at but nevertheless exemplify properties in the actual world. There are well-known difficulties for either sort of view. But, of course, the Meinongian about fictional characters will face the same question about her fictional characters.

Consider a claim from Parsons that he uses as data that the Meinongian can explain (Parsons 1980, p. 32): "Sherlock Holmes is more famous than any living detective." Parsons takes it as a strength of his Meinongian theory that this sentence comes out true in virtue of having Sherlock Holmes (a nonexistent entity) stand in relations to living detectives. But the independence actualist can say the same thing: This sentence comes out true in virtue of Holmes standing in relations to various living detectives.

I think we can see how the independence actualist may mirror what the Meinongian says about fictional characters.[6] However, the independence actualist has fewer entities in her ontology, and those she omits are particularly objectionable. So I conclude that its ability to account for fictional characters offers a third reason to prefer independence actualism to Meinongianism.

Thus, we may see that the three principal sorts of reasons that Meinongians give for being a Meinongian—proper treatment of intentional verbs, negative existential sentences, and fictional character discourse—do not favor Meinongianism over independence actualism. Furthermore, the independence actualist has fewer, and fewer objectionable, entities in her ontology than has the Meinongian. Thus, we may see that we have a *prima facie* reason to accept independence actualism over Meinongianism if we want to embrace the independence thesis.

5

"Exists" as a Predicate

A book on existence is bound to have a chapter on the question of whether "existence is a predicate" and related matters. This is that chapter. In this chapter I want to focus on the question of the semantic functioning of "exists." There has been discussion of the semantics of "exists" and its cognates at least as far back as early modern philosophers like Berkeley, Hume, and Kant.[1] These discussions often center on whether "exists" properly should be considered to be a predicate of some sort. I want to consider this question again, nearly a quarter-way through the twenty-first century. The chapter will proceed as follows. First, I will set out clearly the terms and parameters of our examination of the semantics of "exists" and its status as a predicate. Next I will explicate the two principal sorts of views—the first- and second-order views—that have been espoused over the past three hundred years concerning the semantic functioning of "exists." In the process of this, I will consider reasons for and against each of these views. In the last part of the chapter, I will set out what I think the central considerations ought to be in deciding between the two views. I will argue that either view faces a problem with accounting for the truth of negative existential propositions. As we have seen, the independence actualist has a story to tell about those.

5.1 Terms and Parameters

It is not immediately clear what it is for existence to be a predicate or what one denies when one denies that it is a predicate. For our purposes, when we ask whether existence is a predicate, we will focus our inquiry on a specific class of sentences. These are sentences of the form ⌜N exists⌝, where ⌜N⌝ is some rigid singular term (e.g., a name, demonstrative, or pure indexical).² We will call these sentences "singular sentences." So we want to know whether "exists" as it appears in ordinary singular sentences is a predicate. What does that mean? To say that existence is a predicate in a sentence of the form ⌜N exists⌝ is to say something about the semantic functioning of "exists" and, more broadly, about the sorts of propositions that are expressed by singular sentences. No one denies that "exists" is a predicate in the grammatical sense; obviously it is. And, generally, people who say that existence isn't a predicate don't deny that "exists" contributes to the truth conditions of well-formed sentences it appears in. (At least they shouldn't deny this.) What they mean when they say that existence isn't a predicate is that "exists" isn't a first-order predicate like "is a car" or "is blue" are.

In *Word and Object* we have from Quine an intuitive statement of how the grammatical parts of sentences like singular sentences contribute to the truth conditions of the entire sentence. He says,

> The basic combination in which general and singular terms find their contrasting role is that of predication: "Mama is a woman," or schematically "a is an F" where "a" represents a singular term and "F" a general term [predicate]. Predication joins a general term and a singular term to form a sentence that is true or false according as the general term is true or false of the object, if any, to which the singular term refers. (Quine 1960, p. 96)

This intuitive way of thinking of the roles of singular terms and general terms in determining whole-sentence truth conditions holds for normal predicates like "is a car" or "is blue." The question we are concerned with here is whether it holds for "exists."

When I say "Rome exists," am I picking out an object with "Rome" and putatively saying something about it, in the way I do when I say "Rome is a city?" More precisely, is a sentence like "Rome exists" true or false in the same sort of way a sentence like "Rome is a city" is true or false? "Rome is a city" is true if the subject term "Rome" refers to an object and the predicate "is a city" is satisfied by the referent of the subject term.

People who deny that existence is a first-order predicate, like the predicate "is a city" is, deny that the truth conditions of "Rome exists" are determined in this way. Rather, they think that when I say "Rome exists" I am claiming that something like the *individual concept* or *essence* of Rome is instantiated or exemplified.

We can be even more precise in stating the disagreement between those who think that existence is a first-order predicate and those who think it isn't. In this book we're conceiving propositions as structured entities made up of individuals, properties, and relations that are the semantic contents of parts of sentences. This metaphysics is particularly helpful for characterizing the difference between those who think that existence is a first-order predicate as opposed to those who think that it is a second-order predicate. In particular, those who think that existence is a first-order predicate will disagree with those who think it is not about the makeup of the proposition expressed by singular sentences.³ Those who think that existence is a first-order predicate will claim that a sentence ⌜N exists⌝ expresses a proposition of the form <N, existence>: that is, a proposition with the object referred to by ⌜N⌝ in the "subject" part of the proposition and the property *existence* in the "predicate" part of the proposition. Those who think that existence is a second-order predicate will claim that a sentence ⌜N exists⌝ expresses a proposition of the form <*Individual Essence of N, being instantiated*>: that is, a proposition with an individual essence of the object referred to by ⌜N⌝ (an haecceity or uniquely exemplified world-indexed property [see Plantinga 1974]) in the subject part of the proposition and the property *being instantiated* in the predicate part of the proposition.

We now can state the subject of dispute that we are investigating in this chapter. Does a sentence ⌜N exists⌝ express a proposition of the form <N, existence>? We will call the view it does View 1. Or does it express a proposition of the form <*Individual Essence of N, being instantiated*>? We will call the view it does View 2.⁴ We now turn to discussion of these two views.⁵

5.2 View 1: "Exists" Is a First-Order Predicate in Singular Sentences

This is perhaps the commonsense view about the semantics of "exists." In its surface grammatical structure, "Rome exists" is just like "Rome is a city." The latter involves a predication of an object named by the subject term; so why not the former? Yet, it is surprisingly difficult to find people who defend View 1 explicitly. As we will see, there is no shortage of people who claim that View 1 is false and that the semantics of "exists" is different from that of other predicates. Two prominent philosophers who are proponents of the view that "exists" is a first-order predicate are Nathan Salmon and Peter van Inwagen. In his paper "Existence" Salmon says the view that "the English verb 'exist' (and its cognates) represents, from the point of view of logic, not a first-order predicate of English, but a logical quantifier," is widely recognized to be false (Salmon 1987, pp. 62–3). Salmon goes on to defend View 1 in the rest of "Existence."

In "Being, Existence, and Ontological Commitment," Peter van Inwagen argues that "exists" is univocal. In doing so he draws on Frege's insight that to say that there is something F is to say that the number of Fs is not zero. But he denies that he is thereby committed to saying that "exists" is a second-order predicate.

> When one says "Horses are ungulates" or "Horses have an interesting evolutionary history," one is obviously making a statement about horses and not about the concept horse ... My argument for the univocacy of existence, therefore, does not presuppose that "exists" is a second-level predicate, a predicate of concepts rather than objects, a view that I in fact reject. (Van Inwagen 2014a, p. 62)[6]

Thus, though the explicit defenders of View 1 are few, their number is not zero. We turn to the question of why might someone think that View 1 is true.

5.2.1 Arguments for View 1

Why might someone think that "exists" is a first-order predicate? The principal argument one sees among defenders of View 1 is that we are *able* to treat it as a first-order predicate, and as a result, we *should* treat it as a first-order predicate. For instance, immediately after rejecting the view that "exists" is not a first-order predicate but a quantifier (quoted earlier), Salmon continues:

> Any number of commentators have noted that the term "exists" is fully and completely definable in formal logic as a first-order predicate of individuals, using standard, actualist, Frege-Russellian existential quantification. Its

definition (which also employs the logical notions of identity and abstraction but nothing more) is the following:

(λx)(∃y)[x = y].

Less formally, the English word "exists" may be regarded as being defined by the phrase "is identical with something," or more simply, "is something." (Salmon 1987, p. 63)

His reasoning in this part of "Existence" is that we are able to treat "exists" as a first-order predicate; so why wouldn't we?

William Vallicella (2002, pp. 57–8) argues that this reasoning that we get from the likes of Salmon does not work. He contends that this sort of account is circular. When someone like Salmon says that to exist is to be identical with something, which somethings are we talking about? It has to be existing somethings. But then we're presupposing existence in our account of existence, which is circular.

But people like Salmon aren't giving us an analysis of existence. Rather, Salmon and others are making merely a semantic point: They're just trying to specify the semantic contribution of "exists" to sentences. Their claim is that the logical form of sentences with "exists" in it will be, or at least can be, structurally like that with other one-place predicates. Vallicella is perhaps right that if Salmon et al. were trying to give a reductive analysis of existence, they would be reasoning in an improper way. But they aren't trying to do that.

Barry Miller (2012), in a book-length defense of the view that "exists" is a first-order predicate, also argues that because we can treat existence as a first-order predicate, we should. In this work he spends two chapters attacking arguments that "exists" must be a second-order predicate. Having (to his mind) vanquished these arguments, he begins his chapter 3 having taken himself to have established that "exists" is a first-order predicate.

We get another argument for thinking that "exists" is first order in "Existence" (Salmon 1987, pp. 58 ff.). There he suggests that the success of the cogito in Descartes's *Meditation 2* depends on thinking that existence is a first-order predicate. Salmon says that the cogito "has always struck me as an excellent example of philosophy at its shining best" (Salmon 1987, p. 62). But why does thinking that the cogito establishes the existence of the person engaging in it commit one to View 1? His reasoning is something like this.

When I assert the sentence "I exist," I am directly attributing existence to me, myself. And thus, I am saying, *de re*, of myself that I exist. Thus, "exist" in this case is first order.

But this reasoning by itself doesn't show that "exist" is first order in the sentence "I exist." Suppose, as it seems correct to say, that with the cogito I am *de re* attributing existence to myself. Saying this is consistent with thinking that when I utter the sentence "I exist," I am expressing a proposition of the form <*Individual Essence of Me, being instantiated*>. Saying that I can, *de re*, attribute existence to myself doesn't commit us one way or another to a view about the meaning of the sentence "I exist." I can fully grasp my own existence in the way Descartes thought he could his own while expressing a second-order proposition when I utter "I exist." Thus, I don't think the success of the cogito gives us good reason to think that View 1 is correct.

5.2.2 Arguments against View 1

What about arguments *against* View 1—against the view that "exists" is a first-order predicate? Most such arguments are simultaneously arguments *for* View 2—that "exists" is a second-order predicate. We will tackle those in the next section. Here I want to note three arguments directly against View 1 and against "exists" as a first-order predicate.

5.2.2.1 Argument 1 against View 1: If "Exists" Were a First-Level predicate, It Would Be Predicable of Everything, and This Is Incoherent

We get this argument from Bertrand Russell in his fifth lecture in "The Philosophy of Logical Atomism." He says in reply to a question asked him during the lecture,

> No, there is not an idea [of existence] that will apply to individuals. As regards the actual things there are in the world, there is nothing at all you can say about them that in any way corresponds to this notion of existence. It is a sheer mistake to say that there is anything analogous to existence that you can say about them. You get into confusion through language, because it is a perfectly correct thing to say "All the things in the world exist," and it is so easy to pass from this to "This exists because it is a thing in the world." There is no sort of point in a predicate which could not conceivably be false.

I mean, it is perfectly clear that, if there were such a thing as this existence of individuals that we talk of, it would be absolutely impossible for it not to apply, and that is the characteristic of a mistake. (Russell 1956, p. 241)

Pretty clearly this isn't a good argument. There are all sorts of properties that every existing object has: *being self-identical, not being a round square, being prime or nonprime*, and so forth. The defender of View 1 thinks that *existence* is one among these. Obviously, we tend to care more about the properties that some objects have and others don't. But that doesn't entail that there aren't properties that every object has.

5.2.2.2 Argument 2 against View 1: From True Negative Existentials

This is perhaps the best-known and main argument against View 1, though it's usually not stated in an explicit fashion. It proceeds in the following manner.

Premise 1: Singular nonexistence predications and singular existence predications should be treated equivalently semantically.
Premise 2: Singular nonexistence predications are not first order.
Conclusion: Therefore, singular existence predications are not first order.

What should we make of this argument's premises? Premise 2 is the usual focus of arguments to the conclusion that singular existence predications are not first order. Here are two similar, though distinct, arguments for Premise 2—that singular nonexistence predications are not first order.
Consider the singular nonexistence claim:

(V) Vulcan does not exist.

"Vulcan" was the name given by Le Varrier (whose earlier postulation of Neptune was correct!)[7] in the nineteenth century to the planet between the sun and Mercury. There exists no such planet. So (V) is true. Suppose that "does not exist" in (V) is a first-order predication. Then (goes the argument) we wouldn't be able to account for the truth of (V), for "Vulcan" does not refer to anything that exists. To see why this should be so, recall Quine's (1960, p. 96) statement of the intuitive first-order truth conditions of a sentence like (V). If it is true, then its subject term refers, and the predicate says something of the referent. But this doesn't occur in the case of (V). So (V) isn't true if "does not exist" is a first-order predicate in (V). So it isn't a first-order predicate in (V). The argument generalizes (we should treat other similar sentences in a semantically equivalent manner), so "does not exist" is not a first-order predicate. Call this *the argument from predication* that singular nonexistence predications are not first order.

There is another argument to the conclusion that "does not exist" is not a first-order predicate. We will call this other argument, *the argument from semantic content* that singular nonexistence predications are not first order. It proceeds as follows. Assume that (V) is true and that "does not exist" is a first-order predicate. If "does not exist" in (V) is first order, then (V) expresses a proposition of the form <v, *nonexistence*>. If v is a constituent of the proposition <v, *nonexistence*>, then v exists. But if (V) is true, then v doesn't exist. Contradiction. Thus, if we have true negative existential sentences, "does not exist" is not first order.

Thus, we have two distinct arguments—the argument from predication and the argument from semantic content—that Premise 2 in the main argument against View 1 is true. We may note here that the independence actualist may resist both of these arguments, and we will return to them at the end of the chapter.

What of Premise 1? Premise 1 rules out, for instance, claiming that singular predications of "exists" are first order while also claiming that singular predications of "does not exist" are second order. This sort of semantic dualism might be a natural view to adopt first-blush: "The problems occur when the object isn't around to predicate nonexistence of. So, we'll just have those cases involve second-order predication, while true cases of predication of existence involve first-order predication. Problem solved." But surely Premise 1 is correct. Suppose there were a semantic difference in the way we treat sentences of the form ⌜N exists⌝ and ⌜N doesn't exist⌝ in that "exists" were first order and "does not exist" second order. Then there would be a difference in the semantics of ⌜N⌝ in each case. For the proposition expressed by ⌜N exists⌝ would be of the form <N, *existence*>, and the proposition expressed by ⌜N doesn't exist⌝ would be of the form <*Individual Essence of N, being instantiated*>. In the first case, ⌜N⌝ is directly referential and introduces the object itself, N, into the proposition. In the second case, ⌜N⌝ isn't directly referential and introduces an individual essence of N into the proposition. But surely it can't be that the semantics of names, demonstratives, etc. differ depending only on whether they appear in existence or nonexistence contexts. So we should think that "exists" and "does not exist" should be treated equivalently in terms of order.

5.2.2.3 Argument 3 against View 1: From the Vicious Circularity of Existence

William Vallicella (2002, pp. 42 ff.) gives a series of arguments that a position like View 1 is false. I want to focus on his principal argument here. (The other arguments are similar to his principal argument.) His principal argument proceeds as follows. If "exists" is a first-order predicate, then N instantiates the property *existence* and exists in virtue of instantiating *existence*. But N must already exist to instantiate *existence*—only existing objects exemplify properties. So we arrive at a vicious circularity if we say that "exists" is a first-order predicate. Vallicella characterizes the circularity: "[O]ne would then be saying that a exists in virtue of a's instantiating existence, even though a can do no such thing unless it already (logically, not temporally) exists" (2002, pp. 42ff.).

What should we say about this argument? It trades on two key elements. First, there seems to be a general principle: If an object x is F, it is F in virtue of exemplifying *being F*. Its exemplifying *being F* is the ground of its being F. Second, only existing objects exemplify properties.

Both of these assumptions can be questioned. First, as we have seen (and as we will discuss further at the end of the chapter), one may reject the claim that only existing objects exemplify properties. However, even if one does reject this claim, one still has to acknowledge that *existence* is not a property that can be exemplified without the exemplifier existing (even if others can). Thus, it might seem that Vallicella's main point remains: To exemplify this particular property—*existence*—x has to exist. But once we deny that existence is prior to predication, it's not at all clear that we can generate the problematic circularity. It is true that anything that exemplifies *existence* must exist. But we might insist that it exists in virtue of exemplifying *existence*, rather than that it must "already" exist to exemplify *existence*.

What of the other main element in Vallicella's argument? This is the claim that if x is F, it is F in virtue of exemplifying the property *being F*. Obviously, someone who is a nominalist about properties will reject this argument. But let's set this aside for now and continue to speak as though there are properties. There is a burgeoning literature on concepts like "grounding" and "fundamentality."[8] That metaphysicians discuss these sorts of concepts is natural; metaphysical discourse is shot through with them. The argument for this second element in Vallicella's argument will presumably come in the context of a larger discussion of grounding and truthmaking. In this discussion, one may claim that an object's being a particular way is to be explained by or grounded in the properties it exemplifies. (Presumably this account will apply at the level of properties, and their properties, and so on; though one may get worried that some of the grounding at some point ought to be done by the way something is, full stop.) It's not obvious to me that we should think that the way a thing is to be grounded in property exemplification rather than the other way round.[9] (This is particularly so if we say that grounding at some point is done by the way a thing is.) One can be a Platonist about properties while rejecting these sorts of claims about grounding taking place in property exemplification; there are other routes to Platonism.

But suppose one is attracted to the view that property exemplification grounds the way things are. And suppose one accepts the claim that existence precedes property exemplification. Does that mean that one must give up View 1? Perhaps not. Maybe one could treat *existence* as a special sort of case when it comes to properties' grounding the way things are. One could maintain that something is red in virtue of exemplifying *being red*, that something is a car in virtue of exemplifying *being a car*, and so on. But one might maintain *existence* is a special sort of property, even if one thinks that View 1 is correct. This might be so particularly if one maintains that only existing entities have properties. Perhaps *existence* is the one property that doesn't explain that an object x is the way it is. If it is in some sense presupposed by any predication at all, perhaps one might say that it is the one property for which it fails that an object is F because it exemplifies *being F*.

5.3 View 2: "Exists" Is a Second-Order Predicate in Singular Sentences

View 2 has had many proponents. Indeed, it has been taken to be obviously correct by many philosophers. I want to look at statements from some of the philosophers who have defended View 2 or have said things that are in the spirit of View 2. Then we will turn to arguments for View 2 and some considerations against it.

Descartes thought that existence was contained in the idea of every object. "Existence is contained in the idea or concept of everything because we can conceive nothing except as existent" (Descartes 1955, Replies II, Axiom X; [52], p. 57).[10]

Both Berkeley and Hume thought that there was nothing more to thinking of an object as existing than thinking of the object. Both denied, in particular, that we have any distinct idea of existing. In his *Commonplace Book*, Berkeley writes,

> Strange it is that men should be at a loss to find their idea of Existence; since that (if such there be distinct from perception) it is brought into the mind by all the ways of sensation and reflection, methinks it should be most familiar to us and we best acquainted with it.
>
> This I am sure, I have no idea of Existence, or annext to the word Existence. And if others have that's nothing to me; they can never make me sensible of it; simple ideas being incommunicable by language. (Berkeley 1930)

Hume echoes Descartes in the first book of the *Treatise*:

> The idea of existence, then, is the very same with the idea of what we conceive to be existent. To reflect on any thing simply, and to reflect on it as existent, are nothing different from each other. That idea, when conjoined with the idea of any object, makes no addition to it. Whatever we conceive, we conceive to be existent. (Hume T I.II.VI 1981, p. 66)

It is not clear how to square Hume's claim here with his claim elsewhere that we can conceive of anything as not existing.

Hume's statement here anticipates Kant's famous statements about existence. Indeed, perhaps no philosopher's views on existence's being a predicate are more often noted than those of Kant. In the *Critique of Pure Reason* he says,

> "Being" is obviously not a real predicate, that is, it is not a concept of something which could be added to the concept of a thing. It is merely the positing of a thing, or of certain determinations, as existing in themselves. The proposition "God is omnipotent" contains two concepts, each of which has its object—God and omnipotence. The small word "is" adds no new

> predicate, but only serves to posit the predicate in its relation to the subject. If, now, we take the subject (God) with all its predicates (among which is omnipotence), and say "God is," or "There is a God," we attach no new predicate to the concept of God, but only posit it as an object that stands in relation to my concept ... By whatever and by however many predicates we may think a thing—even if we completely determine it—we do not make the least addition to the thing when we further declare that this thing is. Otherwise it would not be exactly the same thing that exists, but something more than we had thought in the concept; and we could not, therefore, say that the exact object of my concept exists. If we think in a thing every feature of reality except one, the missing reality is not added by my saying that this defective thing exists. (Kant 1965, B626, pp. 504–5)

This passage comes in discussion of the ontological argument. Kant's reasoning here often has been taken to be a refutation of the ontological argument, or at least the ontological argument as given by Descartes in Meditation 5 (though as Plantinga 1966 argues, it is not at all obvious it is). This is striking, for very few people seem to agree on precisely what it is that Kant is saying here, even when they agree that it is a refutation of the ontological argument.

It is reasonable to think that Kant is saying—or at least suggesting—here that "exists" is a second-order predicate. In particular, consider:

> If, now, we take the subject (God) with all its predicates (among which is omnipotence), and say "God is," or "There is a God," we attach no new predicate to the concept of God, but only posit it as an object that stands in relation to my concept.

This sounds like saying that in claiming that God exists, we are saying that there is an instance of the concept of God (see Van Cleve 1999, pp. 187 ff., for discussion)—that is, this sure looks like an endorsement of View 2.

Frege gave View 2 its first clear exposition. In his 1884 *Foundations of Arithmetic* (Section 53), he says,

> By properties which are asserted of a concept I naturally do not mean the characteristics which make up the concept. These latter are properties of things which fall under the concept, not of the concept. Thus "rectangular" is not a property of the concept "rectangular triangle"; but the proposition that there exists no rectangular equilateral rectilinear triangle does state a property of the concept "rectangular equilateral rectilinear triangle"; it

assigns to it the number nought. In this respect existence is analogous to number. Affirmation of existence is in fact nothing but denial of the number nought. Because existence is a property of concepts the ontological argument for the existence of God breaks down. (Frege 1986, pp. 64–5)

We see here that asserting ⌜N exists⌝ is to assert that there are more than zero instances of the concept N. This, one can see, is equivalent to asserting the proposition <*Individual Essence of N, being instantiated*>.

Bertrand Russell has a similarly clear and also influential statement of View 2. In his fifth Lecture on Logical Atomism (from 1918), Russell says,

When you take any propositional function and assert of it that it is possible, that it is sometimes true, that gives you the fundamental meaning of "existence." You may express it by saying that there is at least one value of x for which that propositional function is true. Take "x is a man." There is at least one value of x for which this is true. That is what one means by saying that "There are men," or that "Men exist." Existence is essentially a property of a propositional function. It means that that propositional function is true in at least one instance. (Russell 1956, p. 232)

After Frege and Russell, many thought that View 2 was clearly correct. Thus, Rudolph Carnap in "The Elimination of Metaphysics" says,

Perhaps the majority of the logical mistakes that are committed when pseudo-statements are made [by metaphysicians], are based on the logical faults infecting the use of the word "to be" in our language ... The second fault lies in the form of the verb in its second meaning, the meaning of existence. The verbal form feigns a predicate where there is none. To be sure, it has been known for a long time that existence is not a property (c.f. Kant's refutation of the ontological proof of the existence of God). But it was not until the advent of modern logic that the full consistency on this point was reached: the syntactical form in which modern logic introduces the sign for existence is such that it cannot, like a predicate, be applied to signs for objects, but only to predicates. (Carnap 1959, pp. 73–4)

We get a very clear statement of View 2 from L. S. Stebbing in *A Modern Introduction to Logic*:

This distinction between the way in which properties and the way in which individuals may be presented leads us back to the question as to what is involved in the affirmation of existence. With regard to an individual which is presented and could be named or demonstratively indicated, it is meaningless to assert that it exists … if "exist" be used in the sense it is significant to say "lions exist" … For "Lions exist" means "the property of being a lion belongs to something" … Individuals do not belong in this fundamental sense of belonging to which is involved in the analysis of general propositions. Only properties belong to something. Mr. Russell puts this point by saying that "it is of propositional functions that you can assert or deny existence." … But the language of propositional functions, though convenient, is not essential. What is fundamental, it must be repeated, is the notion of belonging to something. (Stebbing 1950, pp. 160–1)

A. J. Ayer in *Language, Truth and Logic* says,

> But, as Kant pointed out, existence is not an attribute. For, when we ascribe an attribute to a thing, we covertly assert that it exists: So that if existence were itself an attribute, it would follow that all positive existential propositions were tautologies, and all negative existential propositions self-contradictory… (Ayer 1952, p. 43)

Finally, Gilbert Ryle in "Systematically Misleading Expressions" says,

> Since Kant, we have, most of us, paid lip service to the doctrine that "existence is not a quality" and so we have rejected the pseudo-implication of the ontological argument … But until fairly recently it was not noticed that if in 'God exists' existence is not a predicate (save in grammar) then in the same statement God cannot be (save in grammar) the subject of predication. (Ryle 1960, p. 15)

5.3.1 Arguments for View 2

We then see that View 2 has had a number of distinguished defenders. I think that it is not a coincidence that frequently defenses of View 2 arise in the context of talking about the ontological argument. In wanting to resist the argument, people hit on the idea of treating "exists" as a different sort of predicate from predicates like "is perfectly good" or "is all powerful." But why might someone think that View 2 is true? There are, I think, two main reasons that people give for thinking that View 2 is true. (Again, often reasons aren't given; rather, the view is stated as though it is obviously correct.) The first reason is one that we've already seen: denying View 1 and accepting View 2 affords a straightforward treatment of negative existentials without resorting to nonexistent objects. Even if Vulcan doesn't exist, we may maintain the individual concept of Vulcan or the property *being Vulcan* does exist. So I can express complete propositions with utterances of the sentence "Vulcan doesn't exist." We will return to this issue in the last section of the chapter.

A second reason that one might think that View 2 is true has to do with the fruits of treating "exists" as a quantifier. The developments in logic and metaphysics as a result of Frege's (and Peirce's) discovery of predicate logic have been significant. The developments in metaphysics as a result of taking seriously truthmakers for existentially quantified sentences in one's metaphysical theories also have been great (see Van Inwagen 2014b for discussion). Philosophers believe in all sorts of things—numbers, fictional characters, propositions, properties, and so on as a result of what they take to be ineliminable existential quantification over them. It is natural, then, to take "exists" to be a second-order predicate.

But one can take seriously developments in philosophy as a result of applying lessons from predicate logic while denying View 2. View 2 is a claim about the semantics of "exists" in singular sentences. One could claim that "exists" in singular sentences is first order while maintaining that "exists" in other contexts, for example, "cars exist" and "trees exist," is second order. The developments in metaphysics from taking existential quantification seriously would still be open to someone who held this sort of view. One could say that "exists" in non-singular contexts expresses the existential quantifier of first-order logic. One then could look at the types of things over which one quantified ineliminably, and those would be things that one would accept in one's ontology. Developments in philosophy post-Frege by themselves don't require one to deny View 1.

5.3.2 Arguments against View 2

These two motivations for View 2, though stateable succinctly, have been powerful motivators in bringing about belief in View 2. What *problems* have people found with View 2?

5.3.2.1 Moorean Objections to View 2

G. E. Moore gives two quite famous objections to View 2. Moore (1959, p. 122) argues that accepting View 2 entails that if one points at a tiger and says "this exists," the sentence one utters expresses no proposition at all—it is meaningless. He contrasts "this exists" with "this growls," which does express a proposition. The second objection builds on the first. If "this exists" doesn't express a proposition, neither does "It is possible that this might not have existed." But surely, if I utter this sentence, what I utter is meaningful.

The assumption here is that if "this exists" is meaningless, then "this doesn't exist" is meaningless as well. This seems right; indeed, "this doesn't exist" seems a better candidate for difficulty with meaning than does "this exists." But why is the defender of View 2 committed to the view that "this exists" is meaningless? Moore doesn't say. But we may be able to ascertain what he's thinking. He notes that Russell is committed to the view that "this exists" is meaningless, and he says that Russell rightly thinks that it follows from the view that "exists" is a second-order predicate. Perhaps, then, the idea is this. Russell counts demonstratives like "this" and "that" as logically proper names—as names that are directly referential in introducing the referent of the term into the proposition (Russell 1917, pp. 216 ff.; Russell 1956, p. 201). Russell seems to think that, rather than "exists" in "this exists" expressing a first-order property, the overall expression is somehow ill-formed (see Russell 1917, pp. 174–5). This is a consequence of the status of "this" as a logically proper name, Russell thinks.

Further evidence that Moore is thinking of Russell's views on logically proper names here is that it explains why in the course of discussing Russell on the meaningfulness of "this exists" he has a fairly lengthy discussion of "this" referring to sense data (Moore 1959, pp. 123–5). One could treat this as a disconnected aside (Williams 1981, p. 82). But it makes sense in the context of his discussion of Russell on the semantics of "exists." He has in mind Russell's views on logically proper names.

Moore, then, seems to attribute Russell's views about logically proper names and the corresponding semantics of sentences like "this exists" to the defender of a view like View 2. But there is no reason why someone couldn't accept View 2 while rejecting Russell on logically proper names. In particular, one could say that the sentence ⌜N exists⌝ expresses a proposition <*Individual Essence of N, being instantiated*> while accepting the view that "this exists" typically does express a proposition, even in Moorean-type cases. Thus, Moore is incorrect in asserting that View 2 entails that "this exists" doesn't express a proposition.

5.3.2.2 McGinn's Objections to View 2

In *Logical Properties*, Colin McGinn (2000, ch. 2) gives a number of arguments against View 2. I want to examine three of his arguments here.

McGinn says,

> [T]o analyze the existence of a property we need another property that the first one instantiates, and so on ad infinitum. Not only is it doubtful that there always are these further properties, but also we will not succeed in getting any of them to exist without the existence of further ones that raise the same question. Intuitively the existence of a property is intrinsic to it; it is not a matter of some relation that the property stands in to some other property of which it is an instance. And if we construe it as such a relation, then we generate a vicious regress, as each new property raises the question of its own existence. …
>
> No property then will be able to exist unless a whole infinite series exists. But there is no such series, and anyway it would never get off the ground because of the regress. In effect, the orthodox [second order] view makes it impossible to attribute existence to properties. This would have to be declared ill-formed and meaningless (not merely false). (McGinn 2000, pp. 24–5)[11]

This strikes me as not a great argument. Why are we supposed to think that a vicious regress is created for the proponent of View 2? Return to our singular sentence, ⌜N exists⌝. If "exists" here is second order, then the proposition that the sentence expresses will have something like the property *being N* in it. And one may maintain that *being N* exists if it is part of the proposition. Moreover we can grant that *being N* itself has an individual essence, *being being N*, and *being being N* also exists. Correlated with this new individual essence, there must be another true proposition: <*being being N, being instantiated*>. But, of course, we're not committed to expressing or entertaining propositions with these higher-order essences in them when we claim that ⌜N exists⌝ involves higher-order predication. We could do so. I just did go on to say that *being N* exists, and thus now I am entertaining the proposition <*being being N, being instantiated*>. But typically I wouldn't entertain these higher-level propositions. And to assert "exists" in ⌜N exists⌝ is second order, I don't need to entertain these higher-level propositions.

In this reply to McGinn, I am accepting that there are things like essences of essences, and essences of essences of essences, and so forth.[12] But what's the problem with that? At the very least, we have no argument from McGinn that there is something problematic about that series. So far as I can tell, then, a problem for View 2 arises only if to entertain the proposition expressed by ⌜N exists⌝, or to say that "exists" in ⌜N exists⌝ is second order, we need to express or at least entertain higher-level propositions involving higher-order essences. But there's no reason to think that's the case.

Now maybe McGinn thinks that there is a vicious regress if one claims that what grounds the existence of a property like an individual essence is its having a particular relation to another property, like its exemplifying its own individual essence. This regress does indeed seem to be problematic. But the proponent of View 2 is not committed to this sort of claim about grounding. View 2 is a claim about the semantics of "exists" and not about the grounding of property exemplifications in other property exemplifications. Indeed, one could think that grounding goes the other way—that a exemplifies *being F* because a is F and on up—in the way Dixon (2018) sets out.

It's also not clear to me what McGinn's claim that *existence* is intrinsic to properties amounts to. Whatever it is, saying that "exists" is second order is a semantic claim. It's a claim about propositions expressed by sentences of the form ⌜N exists⌝. It doesn't deny the intrinsicality of *existence*.

We get a second argument from McGinn two pages later. There he says,

> The problems of analysis for [View 2] are made vivid by the sentence "something exists." This is a perfectly meaningful and true sentence, which follows from such sentences as "Venus exists," but should itself not exist according to the orthodox view. For it is not paraphrasable within the terms of that view, there being no predicate around to pin the instances on: what property are we saying is instantiated here? (McGinn 2000, p. 27)

This also strikes me as not a great argument. It is obvious how the defender of View 2 should render "something exists": "$\exists x(x=x)$." But "what property are we saying is instantiated here?" No particular property. Or at least none in the way we are when we say "Rome exists." View 2 is a view about the semantics of "exists" in sentences of the form ⌜N exists⌝. But of course, "something exists" is not of that form. It has as its grammatical subject a quantifier term rather than a rigid singular term. No one who defends View 2 needs to claim that all sentences of the form ⌜T exists⌝, where ⌜T⌝ is any grammatical subject, express a proposition of the form <*being T, being instantiated.*>

McGinn gives a third argument against View 2:

> [This objection] focuses on the requirement that any existent thing should fall under some property or other. This implies that nothing could exist that failed to fall under some property—other than existence obviously. To exist is to be an instance of a property, so necessarily whatever exists has at least one property. This rules out, as a matter of the meaning of "exists," the possibility of what we might call "bare existence"—a thing that exists without having any (further) properties. …
>
> [I]t would have to be contradictory to assert the possibility of bare existence, as in "an instance of a property could be an instance of no property." This is simply because existence is being analyzed as property instantiation, and we could not then go on to say that the existent thing has no properties. (McGinn 2000, pp. 28–9)

One might have thought that entailing that there could not be objects with no properties would be something positive for a view, but McGinn sees a difficulty here for View 2. It is worth noting that, as with the first objection mentioned earlier, McGinn is mixing semantics and metaphysics. View 2 is a semantic claim—it is a claim about the proposition expressed by particular sentences. This is distinct from the claim that "to exist is to be an instance of some property." There is a way to connect these two claims, though, so let's do this in an attempt to strengthen McGinn's point. Take some object x (where "x" is a rigid term) that exists. Grant that we could have asserted that x exists. That means on View 2 that the sentence "x exists" expresses a proposition of the form <*being x, being instantiated*>. So we have in the case of x a property that x has—indeed, uniquely has—*being x*.

All right, then with this proviso, View 2 entails that everything that exists has a property. Thus, there can't be "bare existences." But it entails something even stronger—that each thing has a property that necessarily is instantiated only by it. Of course, this also entails there are no bare existences. It's not clear to me that the proponent of View 2 has anything here to be concerned about, though. Presumably there can't be any bare existences: Necessarily, everything has properties like *being self-identical, being such that it isn't a round square,* and *being the number 9 or being distinct from the number 9.* The view that each object has an individual essence is perhaps more objectionable; though if one thinks that properties are semantic values for predicates and thus there is a property for every non-paradoxical predicate, presumably one will think that there are individual essences.

Perhaps McGinn has a different point here, and this is a semantic point. It is that if I think that View 2 is correct, I think that the sentence "x exists and x has no properties" is contradictory. And surely, this isn't contradictory. But why isn't this contradictory? It's certainly necessarily false. Necessarily everything—x included—has all sorts of properties. Why not then say that when I assert the sentence "x exists and x has no properties" (and in doing so involve x in having a number of properties), I say something contradictory?

One other part of McGinn's objection here is worth remarking on. He says, "[On View 2] existence is ... analyzed as property instantiation." But this isn't exactly right. On View 2, particular sentences are given truth conditions that involve property instantiation. This is a semantic claim and is compatible with the view that existence itself is primitive and unanalyzable. Thus, we shouldn't think of the defender of View 2 as *per se* giving an analysis of existence, though she may, of course, opt to do that, as well.

5.4 Assessment of Views 1 and 2

We have considered at length statements of and arguments for and against Views 1 and 2. What should we say about the truth of Views 1 and 2? I think that the main consideration in deciding between Views 1 and 2 is straightforward, though it is usually overlooked. It is this: The semantics of "exists" in singular sentences of the form ⌜N exists⌝ depends on our theory of the semantics of rigid terms, and in particular names.

Recall our statement of the two views under consideration.

View 1: A sentence ⌜N exists⌝ expresses a proposition of the form, <N, existence>.

View 2: A sentence ⌜N exists⌝ expresses a proposition of the form, <*Individual Essence of N, being instantiated*>.

The view one adopts is tied intimately to one's theory of names. If one thinks that names are directly referential and introduce into a proposition the referent of the name, it is very difficult to see how one avoids accepting View 1. On View 1, the referent of the rigid term appears in the proposition that is expressed by the sentence ⌜N exists⌝. This is a directly referential theory of the functioning of ⌜N⌝. If, on the other hand, one thinks that names express individual essences—either haecceities or world-indexed properties in a more Fregean way—one will be drawn to View 2. On View 2, the semantic content of the rigid term ⌜N⌝ is an individual essence of the object N. So those who are rigidified Fregeans (like Plantinga 1978) about names will be drawn to View 2. I find it striking that in general discussions of whether existence is a predicate, questions of the semantics of names don't, or usually don't, arise. Answers to these questions are central to deciding the semantic functioning of "exists" in singular sentences.

It is worth pointing out that one might follow entailments the other way and take the sorts of arguments we've considered in this chapter as reasons to adopt a particular theory of the semantics of names. Thus, I don't think that we should think of the decision between Views 1 and 2 as resting entirely on one's theory of names. But one cannot settle the question as to which view is correct without considerations about the semantics of proper names.

How does one make decisions about the semantics of proper names? We turn to the sorts of considerations Kripke (1980) raises in his attack on Fregean theories of names. We also consider pro-Fregean arguments, like arguments from semantic self-knowledge and arguments from behavior arising within opaque contexts. This book is not the place to rehash these debates.[13] But one's decision as to who gets the best of them will influence one's assessment of Views 1 and 2.

Earlier in the chapter, I said we would return to the question of negative existentials. We do that now. In particular, I want to argue that adopting View

2 via a broadly Fregean theory of names doesn't help with problems of negative existentials.

It is frequently thought that a consideration in favor of Fregean-type theories of names is their ability to deal with negative existentials. Suppose one were a rigidified Fregean and, as a result, adopted View 2. Then one might say that a virtue adopting View 2 is that one has a way for false existence claims and true nonexistence claims to be meaningful. Why would this be? The rigidified Fregean is able to maintain that rigidified essences exist even when the object that exemplifies them doesn't. So propositions expressed by false existence and true nonexistence claims can be complete. Contrast this with the direct reference theorist who adopts View 1: False existence and true nonexistence claims might seem to be meaningless on this view (and thus are neither true nor false). After all, they don't express complete propositions. (This is the sort of reasoning we find in the argument from semantic content in Section 5.2.2.2.)

But this advantage is illusory, I think. For, suppose we decide that English and other similar natural languages are, *pace* Kripke and others, Fregean. It's not a necessary truth that natural languages are Fregean, though. We could have used names and other rigid terms in a directly referential manner. This is just to say that our sentences with names in them could have expressed the propositions that a direct reference theorist thinks they do. And if we had, we'd have the issues that arise with negative existentials for View 1.[14]

Once we see this, we can see that adopting View 2 over View 1 on the basis of negative existential sentences misses the real problem of negative existentials. That real problem is how singular nonexistence propositions could be true. Arguing for a contingent theory of names doesn't change the fact that these propositions still exist. Similarly, arguing for View 2 over View 1 because one is better able to give truth conditions for negative existential singular sentences on View 2 misses the core of the metaphysical debate. One still has to say something about the truth of the negative singular existential propositions that our language would have expressed if we had spoken in a directly referential manner. Thus, a significant problem remains, whether one advocates View 1 or View 2.

It is here that the independence actualist has something to say. Consider the singular proposition *Vulcan does not exist*. If it exists, it essentially has as a constituent the planet Vulcan. It also is actually true if it actually exists. One might be tempted to reason from these premises to the conclusion that there are no such singular propositions, as Plantinga (1983) does. But suppose one is an independence actualist. Then one could say a number of things that would help to explain the truth of negative existential propositions. First, the independence actualist may insist that "Vulcan" does refer to Vulcan, though Vulcan does not exist. (Recall our discussion in Section 3.6 of how the independence actualist may allow for persistently rigid designation.) This would allow one to reply to the argument from predication in Section 5.2.2.

Second, one could say that the proposition *Vulcan does not exist* exists and is true, even though Vulcan does not exist. To see how this would go, recall the discussion of Sib from Section 3.3. There we saw how the independence actualist could maintain that singular propositions about Sib could exist, with Sib as a constituent of them, even though Sib did not exist. They would exist so long as Sib stood in the requisite propositional composition relations to the rest of the singular proposition. Sib may do this in spite of the fact that Sib does not exist. In the Vulcan case, the independence actualist may say one of two things. First she can allow the proposition *Vulcan does not exist* to exist, in spite of the fact that Vulcan does not exist. Vulcan may stand in the requisite propositional composition relations for there to be a complete proposition *Vulcan does not exist*. This would allow one to address the argument from semantic content in Section 5.2.2.

Third, she may opt for the claim that though *Vulcan does not exist* doesn't itself exist due to the nonexistence of Vulcan, it still can be true. Propositions that don't exist nevertheless may have properties like *being true* or *being false*. As I mentioned Section 3.3 in the Sib discussion, my own preference is for necessarily existing propositions that essentially have their constituents, whether or not those constituents exist.

In this chapter we have considered arguments that tell in favor of taking "exists" to be either first or second order in singular sentences. I have argued that the decision between the first- and second-order views of "exists" ought to turn on our views of the semantics of rigid terms. However, adopting a Fregean view of rigid terms and the second-order view doesn't by itself solve the fundamental metaphysical problems it is thought to solve. The independence actualist, however, has resources to reply to problems of negative existential singular propositions. In particular, independence actualism is a view that may aid the direct reference theorist in replying to problems with View 1.

The issues we have been considering in the last part of the chapter lead naturally to discussion of *existentialism*, the view that singular propositions and haecceities are dependent on the objects they are about. We turn to discussion of existentialism in Chapter 6.

6

Existence and Essence

In this chapter I want to explore the relationship between existence and essence. In particular I want to examine the relationship between individuals and haecceities and individuals and singular propositions about them.

Alvin Plantinga has used the term "existentialism" to mean "existence precedes (or at any rate is not proceeded by) essence" (Plantinga 1979). More precisely, existentialism is the view that quidditative properties (like haecceities) and singular propositions are ontologically dependent on the individuals they are about.[1] We will explore existentialism and what the independence actualist has to say about it and related issues in this chapter.

Here, then, are the questions we seek to answer in this chapter:

Question 1: Are singular propositions dependent on the individuals they are about?

Question 2: Are haecceities dependent on the individuals they are about?

Most philosophers who have considered Question 1 have given an affirmative answer to it. Many think that if Socrates doesn't exist, neither do singular propositions about him (e.g., Adams 1981; Braun 1993; Fine 1985; Fitch 1988; Menzel 1991; Prior 1968; Prior and Fine 1977; Salmon 1998; Williamson 2002). With respect to Question 2, others think (usually in conjunction with their views on Question 1) that haecceities are dependent on the things they are about (e.g., Adams 1981; Linsky and Zalta 1994; McMichael 1983; Menzel 1990). The principal defender of a negative answer to Questions 1 and 2 has been Alvin Plantinga (Plantinga 1983 and various other papers in Plantinga 2003b). Later in the chapter, we will look at length at his main argument for a negative answer to these questions. We turn first to discussion of arguments for answering Questions 1 and 2 in the affirmative or the negative. We begin with the affirmative answers.

6.1 Reasons for Answering the Questions in the Affirmative

The standard reason for answering "yes" to Question 1 is because of a commitment to direct reference, alongside a (often tacit) commitment to serious actualism, or something like it. Consider a singular sentence like

(S1) Socrates is a philosopher.

If we are direct reference theorists, the semantic content of "Socrates"—what it contributes to the proposition expressed by the sentence—is the man Socrates. So the proposition (S1) expresses looks like this:

(P1) <**Socrates**, *being a philosopher*>

where "**Socrates**" indicates that Socrates himself is a constituent of the proposition. Consider a world W1 where Socrates doesn't exist. Then one might think it seems plausible to say that (P1) doesn't exist at W1. Why? Because necessarily (P1) exists only if its constituents do, and Socrates doesn't exist at W1. Many direct reference theorists take it for granted that (P1) wouldn't exist at (W1) and don't bother explicitly setting out an argument that (P1) doesn't. But we do see some philosophers spelling out an argument for this. There is a particularly clear statement of this sort of argument from Timothy Williamson.

> Finally consider …
>
> (3+) Necessarily, if the proposition that P(o) exists, then o exists …
>
> A simple defence of (3+) is based on the Russellian view that the proposition that P(o) is a structured entity of which one constituent is a complex consisting of that dog and the property of barking. On this view, the terms that may replace "o" are directly referential in David Kaplan's sense; the contribution of such a term to the proposition expressed by a sentence in which it occurs is simply its referent. If a structured object has a given constituent, then necessarily the former exists only if the latter is a constituent of it and therefore exists too. Since o is a constituent of the structured proposition that P(o), necessarily, the proposition that P(o) exists only if o exists. (Williamson 2002, pp. 240–1)

We see in this quote from Williamson the role of direct reference and serious actualism (or something like it) in the argument that a proposition like (P1) doesn't exist at a world like (W1): "[T]he contribution of such a term to the proposition expressed ... is simply its referent. If a structured object has a given constituent, then necessarily the former exists only if the latter is a constituent of it and therefore exists too."

G. W. Fitch (1988) states an argument for nonexistent objects from the necessary existence of singular propositions. His argument for this rests on the sort of reasoning for the claim that (P1) doesn't exist at (W1).

> The argument [for nonexistent objects as constituents of propositions] goes as follows: there are some possible circumstances or worlds where John fails to exist. Suppose that w is such a world. Since by hypothesis <j, being P> exists necessarily, it exists at w. But if <j, being P> exists at w then its constituents must in some sense also exist at w. Since John does not really exist at w, John must be, relative to w, an unactualized possible. (Fitch 1988, p. 283)

Of course, one could take this reasoning in the direction of the contingent existence of singular propositions. Then one would conclude that <j, being P> doesn't exist at w.

In "Actualism and Thisness," Robert Adams also argues that singular propositions depend on the objects that they are about.

> A singular proposition about an individual x is a proposition that involves or refers to x directly, and not by way of x's qualitative properties or relations to another individual. This relation is surely part of what makes the proposition what it is; it is essential to the proposition, and the proposition could not exist without being directly related to x. (Adams 1981, p. 12)

We then can see the role direct reference plays in getting to an affirmative answer to Question 1. However, Williamson argues that we should give a "yes" answer to Question 1 even if we aren't direct reference theorists.

> However, (3+) is plausible even independently of the direct reference view. On a Fregean view ... the sense of the demonstrative "that dog" in the present context, but not that dog itself, is a constituent of the proposition expressed in the present context by the sentence "that dog is barking." Even so, how could something be the proposition that that dog is barking in circumstances in which that dog does not exist? For to be the proposition that that dog is barking is to have a certain relation to that dog, which

requires there to be such an item as that dog to which to have the relation. (Williamson 2002, p. 241)

One thing that we might draw from all these arguments is that with a singular proposition there is a fundamental aboutness relation that holds between the proposition and some particular object or objects.[2] In the case of direct reference, the aboutness relation is straightforward: The object is a part of the singular proposition. But Williamson maintains that the relevant sort of aboutness may hold even when the object in question isn't a part of the proposition. And there is an assumption throughout that this relation cannot hold without the object the proposition is about existing. It should be clear what the independence actualist can say about these sorts of cases. When Williamson says, "If a structured object has a given constituent, then necessarily the former exists only if the latter is a constituent of it and therefore exists too," the independence actualist may accept the first part of the consequent and reject the second part. If a proposition has an object as a constituent, then the proposition exists only if the object is a constituent of it. But objects may be constituents of propositions even when the object doesn't exist. This fact will form the backbone of a defense of direct reference that we will consider throughout this chapter.

So we see why someone might answer Question 1 in the affirmative. What of Question 2? Why might someone answer it in the affirmative? There is not as much discussion in the literature of Question 2 as there is Question 1. Nevertheless, we do find at least four relevant arguments given. We find two of these from Robert Adams. Here is a passage from "Actualism and Thisness":

> It is hard to see how an actualist could consistently maintain that there is a thisness of a non-actual individual. For if there were one, it would be the property of being identical with that individual. To be the property of being identical with a particular individual is to stand, primitively, in a unique relation with that individual ... [M]y thisness could not exist without being mine ... So if there were a thisness of a non-actual individual, it would stand, primitively, in a relation to that individual. But according to actualism non-actual individuals cannot enter primitively into any relation. It seems to follow that according to actualism there cannot be a thisness of a non-actual individual. (Adams 1981, p. 11)

To begin, we should note the assumption that actualism entails serious actualism. I have argued in this book that it doesn't. I think there are two different sorts of arguments we can mine from Adams's text here. First, note his use of "thisness" in place of "haecceity." If one thinks of an haecceity is the property of *being this thing*, how could there be such a property if there isn't the thing in question? How can there be a thisness if there is no this? A thisness is a sort of an haecceity trope in this regard.

There is a second, similar argument we can take from Adams's text. This is that an haecceity essentially stands in a relation to the individual it is about, and serious actualism says that anything that stands in a relation exists. Now, one may argue that this relationship is the this–thisness relationship just discussed. But one might think that it holds even if one isn't thinking of haecceities in terms of thisnesses. An haecceity is a unique sort of property, primitively tied to the individual who exemplifies it. That sort of property might be thought to be dependent on the existence of the individual who exemplifies it.

A third argument against unexemplified haecceities stems from the idea that haecceities have individuals as parts. If we think that haecceities are like singular propositions in their being directly about an object, we may want to say that haecceities have individuals as parts in the same way singular propositions do. If we say that they do have individuals as parts, we may go on to say that they depend on individuals the way that singular propositions do. Thus, there can't be haecceities that exist that are unexemplified, for they'd not have the individual that they are about as part of them.

There is a fourth argument that one finds against unexemplified haecceities. That is that accepting unexemplified haecceities is tantamount to accepting Meinongianism, which is to be avoided. The criticism is that with a view like Plantinga's (Plantinga 2003a), unexemplified haecceities play much the same role that nonexistent possible objects do on a Meinongian view. Indeed, in the (Plantinga-endorsed) semantics for the metaphysics from Plantinga (2003a), Jager (1982) uses necessarily existing essences in place of the stock of *possibilia* one gets from variable-domain Kripke models. Alan McMichael (1983) makes just this criticism of Plantinga:

> This objection to unexemplified Haecceities is no isolated intuition. Once Plantinga's Haecceitism is fully spelled out, we can see that it bears a striking structural resemblance to the possibilist theories we have rejected. In place

of every nonactual possible object, there stands an unexemplified Haecceity. Indeed, Plantinga's Haecceitist semantics is isomorphic to the usual Kripke semantics. The Kripke semantics is, on the face of it, a possibilist semantics, since we can identify within it a set of all possible objects, actual and nonactual.

This isomorphism is one of the signs that Plantinga is having trouble with the actualist program. Another sign is that he has departed from the usual actualist basis. Typically the actualist reduces worlds to existing individuals, general properties, and general relations. To introduce primitive properties each of which is specific to some non-actual object seems tantamount to acceptance of Meinongianism. Yet this is precisely what Plantinga does. (McMichael 1983, p. 61)

Christopher Menzel makes the same sort of criticism of Plantinga's view:

A traditional platonic understanding of properties—I would argue the dominant one—is that, at the most basic level, properties are what diverse but similar particulars have in common. That properties are, in the first instance, general, they are universals. But on this understanding there seems no justification for purely nonqualitative essences at all, since they are neither general themselves, nor logic compounds of general properties and relations. There is little enough to distinguish purely nonqualitative essences from concrete possibilia save a thin actualist veneer. In light of this understanding of properties that too is stripped away, and haecceitism of this variety collapses into possibilism. (Menzel 1990, p. 366)

What should we make of these four arguments for an affirmative reply to Question 2? I should say up front that it's not important to my project that there be uninstantiated haecceities. Plantinga uses uninstantiated haecceities to stand in for *possibilia*. But where Plantinga will use an unexemplified essence, and the Meinongian a nonexistent object, the independence actualist has use of an object's having properties and standing in relations, though it doesn't exist. So, I assess these four arguments as a nonpartisan. With that caveat, I'm not persuaded by the arguments that they don't exist necessarily, so I'm inclined in the direction of Plantinga's view of haecceities.

Let's begin with the first argument we take from Adams. Consider the haecceity of the table I'm writing at, *being this table in front of me*. Adams asks, how could this property exist if the table didn't? Well, what precisely is the problem with it existing even though the table doesn't? Maybe I couldn't grasp the haecceity if the table didn't exist. Furthermore, maybe if I could grasp it, I wouldn't denote it with "being this table in front of me." There are, of course, many different gerund phrases with which I can pick out the same haecceity. Perhaps if we are thinking of a thisness as a sort of trope—an instantiated haecceity—then *that* couldn't exist without the table existing. But of course the instantiation of *being this table in front of me* is the table, and its self-dependence doesn't give us any reason to think its haecceity, *qua* property, can't exist without the table. So I don't see that this first argument from Adams gives us any reason to think that haecceities can't exist unexemplified. To be fair to Adams, he's not there giving a rigorous argument for the object-dependence of haecceities. Rather, he is pointing to the relation between haecceity and object and hoping that the reader will have his intuitions that the haecceity needs the object.

The second argument from Adams is that haecceities are essentially related to the object they are haecceities of. But this is very close to asserting that haecceities can't exist unexemplified and as such doesn't serve as an independent reason for thinking they can't. It is worth noting that the independence actualist may deny that standing in the sort of primitive relation between a thing and haecceity claimed essential here entails the existence of the relata. So even if one insists that the haecceity needs to stand in relations to the object it is an haecceity of, there is conceptual room to argue that it can do so even if that object doesn't exist.

The third argument for an affirmative answer to Question 2 claims that the haecceity has as a constituent the individual it is an haecceity of. The difference between the haecceity and the object it is an haecceity of is that the former is an abstract object, and the latter (in this case) is a concrete object. This metaphysic blurs this distinction between the two. In this it feels like an attempt to answer the sort of criticism we made of the first argument from Adams: Why precisely can't there be an haecceity that isn't exemplified? A reply might be that the haecceity has as a part the object in question.

There are two concerns one might have with this proposal. First, why should we think that a property can have constituents, much less concrete objects as constituents? Other properties don't have concreta as constituents.[3]

Second, this proposal cuts against two main reasons for believing in haecceities. One reason for believing in haecceities is semantic: Haecceities serve as semantic contents of names and predicates like "is Socrates" and allow one (e.g., Plantinga) to avoid having concrete objects as constituents of propositions. But if the haecceity has Socrates as a part, and the content of "is Socrates" is Socrates' haecceity, then we have introduced concreta into propositions. At that point, why not just have Socrates himself as the content of "is Socrates"? A second reason for believing in haecceities is that they individuate concrete objects (Adams 1981). But they can't do so in a noncircular way if they have concrete objects as parts.[4]

Suppose, though, that haecceities essentially have individual objects as parts. The independence actualist may maintain that this doesn't by itself entail the existence of the individual objects in question. Socrates may stand in the right relation to the rest of his haecceity such that the haecceity can exist, even if Socrates doesn't exist.

What about the fourth argument against unexemplified haecceities—that this view collapses into possibilism or Meinongianism? It is true that in the formal semantics for Plantinga's view in Jager (1982), there is an isomorphism between possible objects and individual essences. But this fact doesn't make Plantinga's own metaphysics in places like Plantinga (1974) and Plantinga (2003a) Meinongian. There are no nonexistent objects on Plantinga's view—that is, in the scope of Plantinga's widest quantifiers, there are only things that exist. Furthermore, names like "Noman," "Vulcan," and "Sib" (see Chapter 3) are nonreferring on Plantinga's account. (They have as semantic contents an essence but don't refer to one.) On a Meinongian account, these names *would* refer, and that reference would be to nonexistent objects. So it's quite clear that a view like Plantinga's on which there are unexemplified haecceities that go proxy in some ways for nonexistent objects doesn't need to be Meinongian, *pace* McMichael and Menzel.

We have looked at reasons for answering Questions 1 and 2 in the affirmative. Let us turn, then, to questions for answering them in the negative.

6.2 Reasons for Answering the Questions in the Negative

Recall the two questions at hand.

Question 1: Are singular propositions dependent on the individuals they are about?

Question 2: Are haecceities dependent on the individuals they are about?

The principal defender of "no" answers to Questions 1 and 2 is Alvin Plantinga. We'll spend most of this section focused on his reasoning for his negative answers. Let us begin with negative answers to Question 2, and then we will return to Plantinga's reasoning for answering Question 1 in the negative.

I want to consider two reasons for answering Question 2 in the negative. The first is from a principle sometimes called "Hume's Dictum": There are no necessary connections between distinct existences.[5] Hume's Dictum and similar such principles have been employed in service of a wide variety of philosophical conclusions: the falsity of nonreductive physicalism, the falsity of ethical nonnaturalism, the extrinsicality of shape, and the possibility of extended simples, among others. We can see how Hume's Dictum may be used in an argument in favor of a "no" answer to Question 2. Suppose my haecceity depends on me for its existence. Then we have a necessary connection between distinct (contingent) existences, which violates Hume's Dictum.[6]

There are at least four things one might say in reply to this argument. The most obvious is to give up existentialism. But suppose one wants to remain an existentialist. What can be said in reply to this argument short of giving up existentialism? One thing the existentialist might say is to reject the core of Hume's Dictum and accept that there are sometimes necessary connections between distinct existences. Though Hume's Dictum is championed by distinguished metaphysicians (including David Lewis), it's not *obviously* true.

Next, the existentialist may claim that the sentiment behind Hume's Dictum is correct, though the formulation of the principle needs to be modified somewhat. Consider a mereological fusion and its parts. The fusion exists just if the parts exist. Or suppose mereological essentialism is true. Then necessarily an object x exists only if its parts do. But, intuitively, these sorts of necessary connections between distinct existences are not the sort of thing that Hume's Dictum is supposed to rule out. So we ought to formulate Hume's Dictum in such a way that there is an allowance for necessary connections between a thing and its parts.[7] Suppose that an haecceity has as a constituent the object that it is the haecceity of. Then this necessary connection between distinct existences might be permissible on this modified version of Hume's Dictum.

We should note, however, that the examples that drove the modification of the Dictum involved mereological parthood. It's not obvious that we should think of parthood in the case of an haecceity and the object that exemplifies it in this same way. Maybe the parthood is like the sort of parthood one gets with a concrete individual and singular propositions about it. But it's dubious *that* parthood is mereological. Perhaps, though, the Dictum should be modified even further to allow there to be haecceities and singular propositions with individuals as constituents. The danger, of course, is that eventually one loses the motivation from the original principle after continually modifying it to avoid counterexamples.

There is a final thing the existentialist might say if she is willing to adopt independence actualism. Suppose, as with the last response, we think of the haecceity as having as a constituent the object it is the haecceity of. Then the independence actualist may claim that the constituency relation holds between haecceity and object even when the object doesn't exist. In this way, we break the necessary connection between distinct existences. The concern I have about this reply is that it's not clear to me in what sense we're left with a full-blown *existentialist* position if one takes this route. It doesn't, of course, entail a Plantinga-like Platonism about haecceities. But the dependence may not be strong enough to satisfy the intuitions that drove the existentialism in the first place.

A second reason for giving a negative answer to Question 2 is the theoretical and explanatory power one gets from doing so. We see in places like Plantinga (1974, 2003a) and Jager (1982) how one can model the original variable-domain Kripke semantics using haecceities. It provides a straightforward way for negative singular propositions to be true, on the assumption that these propositions have haecceities as constituents. In the metaphysics derived from the Kripke semantics (Plantinga 2003a calls this metaphysics the "Canonical Conception"), essences wind up doing much of the work done by objects that exist only in other worlds. As I argued earlier in the book, explanatory power is a *prima facie* reason for favoring a coherent metaphysical picture.

Why might someone answer Question 1 in the negative? The principal argument for this is given by Alvin Plantinga (see Plantinga 1979, 1983, 1985a).[8] Here is a rendering of his argument.[9]

1. It is possible Socrates doesn't exist.
2. Necessarily, if it is possible Socrates doesn't exist, then the proposition *Socrates does not exist* is possibly true.
3. *Socrates does not exist* is possibly true (1–2).
4. Necessarily, if *Socrates does not exist* is true, *Socrates does not exist* exists (from serious actualism).
5. Necessarily, if *Socrates does not exist* is true, then Socrates exists (4, existentialism).
6. Necessarily, if *Socrates does not exist* is true, then Socrates does not exist (intuitively obvious).
7. Therefore, it is possible Socrates exist and not exist (3, 5, 6).

We can see from our contradiction in (7) that at least one of our premises has to be false. Plantinga himself rejects (5) and claims that singular propositions can be true (and thus exist) even though the things they are directly about don't exist. So Plantinga takes this argument to show that we should answer Question 1 in the negative.[10]

There are, though, other ways to reply to this argument. Let us consider each non-derived premise in turn.

Someone like Linsky and Zalta (1994, 1996) or Williamson (2013) will reject (1) in the argument. Socrates exists necessarily, as does everything else. But how do we make sense of the notion that we think and say that Socrates could have failed to exist? There is an alternative in the neighborhood that is supposed to be close to the claim that Socrates could have not existed: that Socrates could have failed to be concrete. *Being possibly non-concrete* is a suitable replacement for the contingency of Socrates, Linsky and Zalta and Williamson say. However, it seems to me (and to most in the literature) that our metaphysic should allow for the truth of (1). It's worth noting that their denial of (1) comes from a methodological commitment on the part of Linsky and Zalta and Williamson to reality's corresponding to certain claims in modal logic. For those of us who don't share that methodological commitment, the denial of (1) likely will not seem plausible.

When considering (2), the distinction between two sorts of truth with respect to a world is often invoked (see, e.g., Adams 1981; Fine 1985; Menzel 1991; Prior 1976; Pollock 1984, 1985; Stalnaker 2010, 2012). Here is Kit Fine invoking this sort of distinction.

> One should distinguish between two notions of truth for propositions, the inner and the outer. According to the outer notion, a proposition is true in a possible world regardless of whether it exists in that world; according to the inner notion, a proposition is true in a possible world only if it exists in that world. We may put the distinction in terms of perspective. According to the outer notion, we can stand outside a world and compare the proposition with what goes on in the world in order to ascertain whether it is true. But according to the inner notion, we must first enter with the proposition into the world before entertaining its truth. (Fine 1985, p. 163)

Robert Adams uses similar language.

> A [possible world] that includes no singular proposition about me constitutes and describes a possible world in which I would not exist. It represents my non-existence, not by including the proposition that I do not exist but simply by omitting me. That I would not exist if all the propositions it includes, and no other actual propositions, were true is not a fact internal to the world that it describes, but an observation that we make from our vantage point in the actual world. ...
>
> Let us mark this difference in point of view by saying that the proposition that I never exist ... is true *at* many possible worlds, but *in* none. (Adams 1981, p. 22; emphasis in original)

Fine's inner truth or Adams truth-in is the ordinary notion of truth in a world that we see from Plantinga (1974). Let's call this sense of truth "truth inside a world."[11] We can define it as follows.

> T_I: A proposition p is **true inside** a world W just if necessarily, if W is actual, p is true.

We aren't, however, given an analysis of Fine's outer truth or Adams' truth-at, which we will call "truth outside a world." (We will return to this fact momentarily.) Rather, we're given a sort of picture to operate with. We evaluate the truth of a proposition from our perspective in the actual world and ask if it is true, regardless of whether it exists there.

How do proponents of the distinction between truth inside a world and truth outside a world think that the distinction bears on our argument? They maintain that there is an ambiguity in (2). (2) can be read either as:

(2') Necessarily, if it is possible Socrates doesn't exist, then the proposition *Socrates does not exist* is **true inside** some possible world.

(2") Necessarily, if it is possible Socrates doesn't exist, then the proposition *Socrates does not exist* is **true outside** some possible world.

The existentialist who avails herself of the truth inside/outside distinction may maintain that (2') is false. And, while (2") is true, it conjoined with (1) doesn't validly yield (3); for (3) as it functions in the argument is a claim about truth inside a world. So, either way the main argument is not sound.

At first our intuitions may balk at the claim that *Socrates does not exist* is not true *simpliciter* if the world in question W (where Socrates doesn't exist) is actual. But we are meant to see that it's *almost true*, or *sort-of true*; *Socrates does not exist* is true *outside* W. And that is supposed to be enough to satisfy the intuition that it's possible that Socrates not exist.

There have been a number of attempts to say what outside truth is. Robert Stalnaker says,

> [Outside truth], in the relevant sense, is just entailment: a proposition is true with respect to a given possible state of the world if and only if that proposition is entailed by the maximal proposition that is that possible state of the world. (Stalnaker 2012, p. 31)

I think we can see that this won't work. Consider a world W where Socrates doesn't exist. Suppose we think of W as a maximal proposition. Suppose also we adopt serious actualism, as we do in Plantinga's argument. Does W entail the proposition *Socrates does not exist*? No, because it's not the case that necessarily, if W is actual, *Socrates does not exist* is true. If W is actual, *Socrates does not exist* doesn't itself exist (and the defender of truth outside a world as distinct from truth inside a world assumes serious actualism). The existentialist may reply, "Yes, it's not true *inside* W. But it is *outside* W." That's fine so far as it goes, but it's not something Stalnaker can say here. He's trying to tell us what outside truth is and can't appeal to it in giving an account of it.

It might be tempting to give an analysis of outside truth in terms of states of affairs that obtain or properties that are exemplified in or "inside" W. The problem, of course, is that the motivation the existentialist has for thinking *Socrates does not exist* is not true inside W will apply to any quidditative state of affairs or property. To give a proper analysis of a singular proposition's being true outside a world in terms of some other abstract object obtaining inside or being instantiated inside a world, the thing the singular proposition is about must show up, quidditatively, in the analysans. When that happens, the existentialist will face questions about the existence of this new abstract object, which was to do the grounding for the fact that the singular proposition was true outside the world in question.

Jason Turner (2005) gives the following conditions for a non-modal proposition p's being true outside a world W. He takes the disjunction of the conditions in each of the three to be necessary for p to be true outside W. (He defines "E!" as follows: E!(a) is true iff $\exists x(x=a)$.)

(C1) If p is true [inside] W, then p is true [outside] W.

(C2) If p="~E!(a)," w is W's world description, and a is not a constituent of w, then p is true [outside] W.

(C3) If a proposition p follows in a negative free logic from propositions true [outside] W, then p is true [outside] W.

(C2) will be the condition we are most concerned with here, for we seek an account of what it is for the proposition *Socrates does not exist* to be true outside a world W. Turner thinks of world descriptions as maximal propositions that describe what happens in a world. In (C2) Turner is availing himself of the notion of a's being a constituent of the world description in question, w. Let's suppose that a in this case is Socrates. If in the actual world α, Socrates is not a constituent of the world description w, then the proposition *Socrates is not a constituent of w* will be true in α. What is the alethic status of this new proposition, *Socrates is not a constituent of w*? First, we can note that it is true inside α; and its truth inside α, the actual world, is supposed to allow it to make *Socrates does not exist* true outside W. Second, we can note that it too is true outside W. Like the proposition *Socrates does not exist*, it won't exist if W is actual. But both accurately characterize W, from our perspective in α. What makes it the case that it is true outside W? We don't have an account in (C2), as (C2) is about negative existential propositions. I suspect Turner would say that it is true outside W because it follows from the proposition *Socrates does not exist*, which is true outside W. An initial concern here might be that the order of explanation is supposed to go the other way round; the proposition about constituenthood in a world story is supposed to explain the outside truth of the negative existential proposition. Perhaps though we could appeal to something else true inside α to explain the truth outside of W of the proposition *Socrates is not a constituent of w*: *Socrates is not a constituent of w is not a constituent of w*. This would give us an account of how, from our perspective in α, various things are true of W.

I think we can see that the disjunction of (C1)–(C3) is not necessary for truth outside a world, though. Consider again the case of Sib.[12] We know Sib doesn't exist in α. Suppose Sib also doesn't exist in W. Then the proposition *Sib does not exist* should be true outside W; it accurately characterizes W from our vantage point in α. But the existentialist presumably must say *Sib is not a constituent of w* is not true inside α, for it doesn't exist in α. So *Sib does not exist* being true outside W is not via (C2). *Sib does not exist* also is not true inside W, as it doesn't exist inside W.[13] Thus, the outside truth of *Sib does not exist* at W is not via (C1). Nor does it follow from a proposition true outside W in a negative free logic; thus, *Sib does not exist* is not true outside W via (C3). Thus, the outside truth of *Sib does not exist* must be explained by some means other than those we find in (C1)–(C3). So the disjunction of conditions in Turner's (C1)–(C3) is not necessary for truth outside a world. Thus, Turner has not given us an analysis of truth outside a world.

Jeff Speaks (2012) attempts to give an analysis of truth outside a world in terms of worlds, in α, having quidditative truth conditions. He construes these truth conditions as properties. The idea is that W actually has the property *being such that if W is actual Socrates does not exist*. This is supposed to secure that *Socrates does not exist* is true outside W. Why? Because were W actual, Socrates would not exist. I have two concerns about this proposal. First, it too has trouble with the Sib case. *Sib does not exist* should be true outside W. But in α W doesn't have the truth condition *being such that if W is actual, Sib does not exist*, for this is a quidditative property and doesn't exist in α by the existentialist's own lights.

Second, note that Speaks's truth conditions are "object-level" and don't involve propositions. So, he's not saying that W has the truth condition *being such that were W actual, the proposition **Socrates does not exist** would be true*. This is the sort of thing only the denier of existentialism, or perhaps serious actualism, could say. But he does accept that the condition Socrates does not exist would hold if W were actual. But surely, W would record this fact with abstracta of some kind—a proposition, presumably—were W actual. How can the condition in the consequent of the truth condition hold inside the world if the requisite proposition isn't true inside the world? Perhaps the idea is that the condition holds outside the world. But then we're clearly not giving a reductive analysis of outside truth, for we're invoking outside truth in the analysis.

Perhaps one might think that I'm being unfair to the existentialist, which the person giving an account of truth outside a world presumably is. For the existentialist, *Sib does not exist* does not exist in α. Isn't there something wrong with my appealing to it in arguing against accounts of outside truth?[14]

In reply, consider what one is trying to do when giving an account of truth outside a world. One starts with the idea that, from our perspective in the actual world, certain propositions will truly characterize other worlds even though they don't exist inside those worlds. Our analysis of outside truth needs to track that idea; it should be able to give an account of all the cases where such a proposition accurately characterizes such a world, regardless of whether it exists inside that world or our world. But we can see that it doesn't give such an account: It doesn't allow for *Sib does not exist* to be true outside W, even though from our perspective in the actual world it ought to be. It is, of course, true that the existentialist will say that *Sib does not exist* does not exist in α. But I'm not asking for it to be true in α; rather, I'm asking for it to be true outside W. That is a datum that an account of outside truth ought to explain.

I suspect there is no noncircular reductive account of truth outside a world (see Davidson 2000, 2007b). The concept may be a perfectly good one, of course. Maybe there just isn't a reductive analysis of it, though we understand it and find it useful to employ. But it would be good to have an analysis of what it is. It is much more complex than other potential primitives for which we may not seek analyses (e.g., modality, truth, existence). Thus, it seems like the sort of thing that should have an analysis, in the way that truth inside a world has an analysis.

Let us see if there is another way to reject our main argument from Plantinga, then. We turn to premise (4),

(4) Necessarily, if *Socrates does not exist* is true, *Socrates does not exist* exists.

The independence actualist may reject (4) in that she may maintain that a proposition can be true in spite of the fact that it doesn't exist. However, I think there is a better way for the independence actualist to attack the argument.

Consider the next premise:

(5) Necessarily, if *Socrates does not exist* is true then Socrates exists.

As we saw in Chapter 3, the independence actualist may say that a singular proposition like *Socrates does not exist* exists even though a constituent of it doesn't exist. Socrates may stand in the requisite propositional composition relations for there to be the proposition *Socrates does not exist* even in worlds where Socrates doesn't exist.

Rejecting (5) would perhaps be a strange sort of "victory" for the existentialist in replying to Plantinga's anti-existentialist argument. Plantinga's argument is designed to show that existentialism is false and that singular propositions exist necessarily. This independence actualist reply that denies (5) allows for negative existential singular propositions to exist necessarily, which is not something that (typically) the existentialist would plump for. It's worth asking, though, why would one embrace existentialism, and why in particular would one embrace that singular propositions are contingent entities that exist only if the objects they are about exist? The usual reason for this is that one accepts direct reference, and one thinks that the referent of a rigid term is a constituent of the proposition expressed by the sentence in which the term occurs. The contingent existence of the singular proposition is a by-product of one's theory of reference and semantics. The contingent existence of singular propositions is not, as it were, the main attraction. Thus, we may view independence actualism as a way of saving direct reference theory from arguments like Plantinga's. The direct reference theorist may maintain that *Socrates does not exist* is a necessary being. It necessarily has Socrates as a constituent, though in some worlds, Socrates exists, and in others, he doesn't. Plantinga's argument pushes in a direction away from direct reference (see Davidson 2000): Plantinga's argument implies singular propositions like *Socrates does not exist* exist even when the object they are about doesn't exist. Thus, concreta aren't constituents of propositions. The independence actualist may retain direct reference and reject premise (5) in Plantinga's argument.

We now have considered reasons for giving affirmative and negative answers to Questions 1 and 2. We turn to a related puzzle from Kit Fine that will serve to illustrate the utility of independence actualism in solving problems in the metaphysics of existence.

6.3 A Puzzle from Kit Fine

In Kit Fine's "Necessity and Non-Existence" (Fine 2005, p. 328), we find the following puzzle.

1. It is necessary that Socrates is a man.
2. It is possible Socrates does not exist.
3. Therefore, it is possible that Socrates is a man and does not exist.

This looks like a valid argument. (1) says that in every possible world Socrates is a man. (2) says that in at least one world Socrates doesn't exist. So in that world, Socrates is a man and doesn't exist.

What about its premises? Fine says we should accept (1) because it is in the nature of Socrates to be a man. (2) is intuitively obvious, he says. So, Fine says, we have an argument that appears to be valid with true premises. Yet, its conclusion is false, he says. This is a puzzle, "whose difficulty and significance has not … been fully appreciated" (Fine 2005, p. 328).

Fine considers two extant replies to this sort of puzzle. The first he takes from Arthur Prior (Prior 1957). According to the Priorian solution, singular propositions are neither true nor false at worlds where the object they are about doesn't exist. Thus, if we take a world where Socrates doesn't exist, the proposition *Socrates is a man* is neither true nor false there. So the inference doesn't go through to the conclusion in (3) if we read (3) as asserting there is a possible world where it is true Socrates is a man and doesn't exist.

We might put the response from Prior in a slightly different way. On this Priorian picture, there are two senses of necessity: There is truth in all possible worlds (strong), and there is not being false in any possible world (weak). There are also two senses of possibility on this picture: There is truth in a possible world (strong), and there is not being necessarily false (weak). (1) is true on a weak reading of the necessity involved and (2) on a strong reading of possibility. That (1) is true only on a weak reading of necessity means that we can't validly derive (3) from (2), which is intended to be true on a strong reading of possibility.

The second reply to the puzzle Fine calls "the standard solution." On it, the first premise is rejected. But something close to (1) is true, that is

(1') Necessarily, if Socrates exists, Socrates is a man.

But of course (1') and (2) don't validly imply (3), and we are able to reply to the puzzle.

Fine finds it implausible that there is the sort of equivocation between premises and conclusion that the Priorian posits in her solution to the puzzle. So Fine rejects the first solution to the puzzle. He finds the second solution problematic because he takes it to be equating x's necessarily having a property with x's having a property in every world in which x exists. But on that account any x winds up existing necessarily.

It seems to me that Fine is right to reject Prior's solution, if only because of its denial of bivalence and the effects that has on one's logic. But I think we can fix the second response to make it more plausible. Suppose we follow Plantinga (1974) and distinguish between an object's having a property necessarily and an object's having a property essentially. An object has a property necessarily just if it has it in every world, and (on the assumption in the standard reply that serious actualism is true) this entails that only necessary existents have properties necessarily. An object has a property essentially just if it has it in every world in which it exists. We then can see that the standard reply may construe the first premise of the puzzle as

(1") Socrates is essentially a man

rather than

(1') Necessarily, if Socrates exists, Socrates is a man.

The advantage here is that there is no suggestion of an analysis of having a property necessarily in (1"), though two claims are otherwise equivalent. That is, if we take (1") to be the proper reading of (1), we're not inclined to give an analysis of having a property necessarily in terms of having a property in every world one exists. As before, once (1) is replaced in our puzzle, there no longer is a valid inference, and the puzzle is resolved.

But doesn't the analysis of having a property essentially entail that Socrates essentially exists? Yes, but that's just what people like Plantinga claim.

> Every object, clearly enough, exists in every world in which it exists; so everything has essentially the property of existing. This is not to be boggled at. Everything has existence essentially; but only some things—properties, propositions, numbers, God, perhaps—have necessary existence, the

property an object has if it exists in every possible world. (Plantinga 1974, p. 61)

Fine would object to this solution in that he thinks that we ought to think that Socrates has the property being a man necessarily. It is part of the nature of Socrates to be a man, and as a result, that he is a man ought to hold in every possible world (Fine 2005, p. 332). It's not obvious to me that properties that follow from one's essence need to hold in every possible world. However, this sort of reasoning is actually supportive of the claims that the independence actualist might make. The independence actualist could accept that (1) is true as stated—true in every possible world, whether or not Socrates exists there. Indeed, the independence actualist could go on to take the Fineian puzzle as sound as stated. There are, indeed, some possible worlds where Socrates doesn't exist and is nevertheless a man. Once one allows objects to have properties in worlds where they don't exist, Fine's argument no longer is so puzzling.[15]

This suggests an important question: How should the independence actualist think of the instantiation of essential properties? Here are three different views one might adopt about essential properties:

1. **Minimal Essentialist View**: An object has its essential properties in every world where it exists and no essential properties in worlds where it doesn't exist (in some of which it has other properties).
2. **Moderate Essentialist View**: An object has its essential properties in every world where it exists and in every world where it has any properties at all.
3. **Maximal Essentialist View**: An object has its essential properties in every possible world.

As with the different grades of independence actualism in Chapter 3, there are views that fall between these three grades of essentialism. Which of the three should the independence actualist adopt? I take it that the Minimal view can be ruled out. If an object has properties in worlds where it doesn't exist, surely among the properties it has should be its essential properties. And the independence actualist's claim is that things may have properties in worlds where they don't exist. So they should have essential properties in those worlds, as well.

The choice, then, is between the Moderate and Maximal views. The advantage of the Maximal view is that it allows one to take seriously the Finean intuition that essential properties should hold of necessity. But it's not obvious to me that the Moderate view takes essential properties insufficiently seriously. It says that any world where an object has any properties, it has all its essential properties. Thus, in any world where we have any predication occurring (whether or not the object exists), the object has its essential properties.

I don't then see a strong motivation for choosing the Maximal over the Moderate view, though if someone had sufficiently Finean intuitions about essence, they might be inclined to choose the Maximal view over the Moderate view.

6.4 The Questions, Again

This chapter is framed around the answering of two questions:

Question 1: Are singular propositions dependent on the individuals they are about?
Question 2: Are haecceities dependent on the individuals they are about?

What should the independence actualist say about each? It is most plausible to me to answer Question 1 in the affirmative, so long as we maintain that propositional dependency relations as manifest in the relations that tie properties and relations together into a proposition may hold even when one of the relata doesn't exist. As I mentioned earlier, I'm inclined in the direction of thinking haecceities exist necessarily. But we should note that this doesn't preclude a "yes" answer to Question 2 if one is an independence actualist. One could say that an haecceity stands in an essential dependence relation to the thing it is an haecceity of, even if that object doesn't exist. Perhaps there is some sort of argument that the dependency relations between haecceity and object are such that each relatum must exist to stand in them, but it's not at all clear how such an argument would go. If one could make such an argument, then I'd be inclined to answer Question 2 in the negative.

7

Robust and Deflationary Meinongianism

In this book I have argued, among other things, that one ought to prefer independence actualism to Meinongianism. That is, I have argued it is preferable to allow objects that aren't in the scope of our widest quantifiers to exemplify properties and stand in relations than it is to have nonexistent objects in the scope of our widest quantifiers. Suppose, though, that you are a Meinongian who is unconvinced by the course of argumentation so far in the book. You are, indeed, set on having nonexistent objects in your ontology. In this chapter I want to offer some friendly advice to the deeply committed Meinongian about what sort of Meinongianism she ought to adopt.

We begin the chapter by setting out two different sorts of Meinongianism, what I will call "Robust" and "Deflationary" Meinongianism. After that, I will place a number of Meinongianisms into the Robust and Deflationary camps. After exploring these different Meinongianisms I will argue that if one is going to be a Meinongian, one should be a Robust Meinongian.

7.1 Two Types of Meinongianism

We begin with characterizations of Robust and Deflationary Meinongianism. The Robust Meinongian thinks that nonexistent objects may exemplify the same sorts of properties and may stand in the same sorts of relations ordinary existent objects exemplify or stand in. Thus, for the Robust Meinongian, nonexistent entities may have shapes and sizes and colors, they may be of a particular species or artifact type, or they may have causal powers to affect other existent or nonexistent objects. Robust Meinongians may disagree as to precisely which properties nonexistent objects may have, though all will agree that they stop short of exemplifying *existence*. The Deflationary Meinongian, by contrast, thinks that nonexistent objects exemplify very few of the types of properties and stand in very few of the sorts of relations that ordinary existing objects exemplify or stand in. For instance, a Deflationary Meinongian might say that nonexistent objects may exemplify only the property *nonexistence*. Or she might say they may exemplify *nonexistence* together with various representation-dependent or Cambridge-style properties or relations such as *being thought of by me* or *being referred to by me*.

We should note that the Robust Meinongian need not say that every nonexistent object exemplifies every property (or its complement) had by ordinary objects. Many Robust Meinongians think that there are *incomplete* objects that will not exemplify various properties or their complements. So the Robust Meinongian may have some nonexistent objects that exemplify few properties. But she will have others that exemplify very many of the sorts of properties exemplified by ordinary existing objects. The Deflationary Meinongian will think that necessarily, there are none of these richly propertied nonexistent objects.

The Robust Meinongian, then, thinks that there are nonexistent objects in the scope of our widest quantifiers, and that these objects may exemplify the same sorts of properties that ordinary, existing objects do. The best-known example of a Robust Meinongian is Meinong himself. Meinong thought that there were many objects that neither exist (as concreta do for Meinong) nor subsist (as abstracta do for Meinong). Rather, these objects are beyond being of any kind. Though beyond being, these objects exemplify properties like *being round, being square, being golden,* or *being a mountain*. Here is Dale Jacquette describing Meinong's view:

> We have seen that for Meinong, even beingless objects, though nonexistent, have Sosein. An object's Sosein … are the properties that determine and individuate intended objects. The round square is the object that has the constitutive properties of being simultaneously round and square. The golden mountain is the intended object that has the constitutive properties of being golden and a mountain. The round square is truly round and square, or has the constitutive properties of being round and square in its Sosein, even though it does not, and, indeed, cannot, exist. (2015, p. 15)

Bertrand Russell launches a series of attacks against Meinong (Russell 1973). In one of his objections he claims that Meinong is committed to there being an object that satisfies any definite description, and thus there being an object that satisfies "the existent round square." Such an object would be a round square that exists. As there isn't (and couldn't be) such an object, Meinong's theory is fatally flawed. In reply, Meinong, particularly in his earlier work, says that the round square, though existent, doesn't exist. Meinong seems to have thought that there were "weakened" versions of properties like *existence* that an object like the round square could have without actually having to exist. How do you get from an object's having the weakened version of *existence* to an object's having the full-blooded version of *existence*? One needs to add what Meinong calls "the modal moment" (see Findlay 1963, ch. IV, for discussion). The modal moment is something like a function from a weakened version of a property to a full-blooded version of the property. (We're not told much more than that. It's not at all obvious to me that this reply makes sense, though working through its details is beyond the scope of this chapter.)

Many of the best-known contemporary Meinongians, such as Terrence Parsons (1980), Richard Routley (2018), Colin McGinn (2000, 2004) and Dale Jacquette (1996, 2015), have followed Meinong's lead in adopting Robust Meinongianism.[1] For each of these philosophers, the golden mountain exemplifies *being golden* and *being a mountain*. Fictional characters like Sherlock Holmes exemplify properties like *being a detective* and *wearing a deerstalker hat*. Here is Jacquette describing this sort of view (we see similar statements from Parsons 1980, p. 18; McGinn 2004, p. 225; and Routley 2018, pp. 31–2).

> A nonexistent object, in a Meinongian semantics, can be a detective, a winged horse, or anything else that thought might freely intend. Sherlock Holmes for a Meinongian, although as much flesh and blood as Richard Nixon, unlike Nixon, does not have real actually existent flesh and blood. No more than, for example, Holmes's left eye is a real actually existent eye, or his violin a real actually existent violin. The fact that Holmes is as much flesh and blood as Richard Nixon is no embarrassment to Meinongian object theory. (Jacquette 2015, p. 280)

Contemporary Meinongians have not followed Meinong's use of the modal moment as a reply to Russell's objection involving the existent round square. Rather, Meinongians like Parsons, Routley, and Jacquette have settled on a distinction between different sorts of properties. This distinction has several names: nuclear versus extranuclear (Parsons), characterizing versus non-characterizing (Routley), and constitutive versus extraconstitutive (Jacquette). (Most of the literature seems to have settled on Parsons's language, so I will adopt it.) How is the nuclear–extranuclear distinction supposed to help with the existent round square problem? The Robust Meinongian who adopts this distinction will claim that for any collection of nuclear properties, there is (read the quantifier in as wide a sense as possible) an object that exemplifies those properties. Properties like existence, however, are not nuclear properties. Thus, this sort of Robust Meinongian is not committed to the claim that there is an object that is round and square and exists.[2]

In Parsons and Routley we aren't given an analysis of what a nuclear property or extranuclear property is. Rather, we are given a rough outline of the sort of property that fits into each category. For instance, we see in Parsons:

> I'll call "exists" an extranuclear predicate, and, in general, I'll divide predicates into two categories: those which stand for nuclear properties, which I'll call nuclear predicates, and the others, which I'll call extranuclear.
>
> Which are which? ... Our historical situation yields a very rough kind of decision procedure for telling whether a predicate is nuclear or extranuclear. It is this: if everyone agrees that the predicate stands for an ordinary property of individuals, then it is a nuclear predicate and it stands for a nuclear property. On the other hand, if every agrees that it doesn't stand for an ordinary property of individuals ... or there is a history of controversy about whether it stands for a property of individuals, then it is an extranuclear predicate and it does not stand for a nuclear property. Of course this "decision procedure" is a very imperfect one. Probably its main virtue is to give us enough clear cases of nuclear and extranuclear predicates for us to develop an intuition for the distinction. (Parsons 1980, pp. 23–4)

We are also given a list of some extranuclear predicates in Parsons. These include "exists," "is mythical," "is fictional," "is possible," "is impossible," "is thought about by Meinong," "is worshipped by someone," and "is complete."

We have a similar characterization in Routley, where he relies on a list of different predicates to help the reader grasp the distinction between nuclear and extranuclear predicates (Routley 2018, pp. 344 ff.).

Jacquette (2015) does provide an analysis of nuclear and extranuclear predicates. He says,

> [U]nlike nuclear properties, where both the property and its complement [may fail] to hold of a given Meinongian intended object, there are only two truth valued possibilities for extranuclear predications. They are either true or false, so that their external negation forms are logically equivalent to their internal predicate complementation forms. (Jacquette 2015, p. 97)

The idea, then, is that with nuclear predications, an object may satisfy neither a nuclear predicate nor its complement. But with extranuclear predications, it follows from the fact that it is false that an object is F that the object is non-F. Why the difference in completeness for the two predications? It is presumably because Jacquette thinks (along with Parsons and Routley) that there can be incomplete objects: Objects that are such that for some (nuclear) property F, they exemplify neither F nor its complement. So, for example, a nonexistent object may exemplify neither *being blue* nor *being nonblue*. This may be the case if an object is designated by a description that includes no information about the color of the object. For Jacquette, nuclear properties are possibly such that neither they nor their complement is exemplified by an object. Extranuclear properties are such that necessarily, either they or their complement is exemplified by an object.

We should note that this characterization of the nuclear–extranuclear distinction doesn't allow for a version of Meinongianism on which there are only complete objects. To understand this sort of Meinongianism, consider how an epistemicist thinks about meanings of vague predicates. For an epistemicist, a vague predicate expresses a particular property that is its semantic content.[3] This is the case even if we aren't sure precisely which property is expressed by the predicate. (Indeed, this lack of knowledge is the source of vagueness in natural language.) Suppose one thought of nonexistents in a way analogous to the way the epistemicist thinks of the semantic contents of vague predicates. Then, when I designate an object with "the golden mountain," I designate a particular nonexistent object with a complete set of exemplified properties. The nonexistent mountain I pick out has a height, mass, and a circumference, even if I am not able to say what they are. Suppose, further, necessarily all objects (existent and nonexistent) are like the referent of "the golden mountain" in that that they have a complete set of properties. Then Jacquette's criterion wouldn't allow us to distinguish between nuclear and extranuclear properties. This would close off the nuclear–extranuclear distinction as a way of replying to the existent round square problem.

One might have thought that the nuclear–extranuclear distinction should be independent of the possibility of incomplete objects. Conceptually, it seems to be. If we started with the intuitive (if non-rigorous) sorting of nuclear and extranuclear properties that we see in Parsons, there would seem to be nothing wrong with my adopting a nuclear/extranuclear Meinongianism on which necessarily all objects are complete. However, if Jacquette is right in his analysis of the nuclear–extranuclear distinction, this is false. This suggests to me that Jacquette's analysis is not correct; it is at best extensionally adequate on the assumption that there are or could be incomplete objects with the right distribution of properties.

Whether or not Jacquette's analysis of the nuclear–extranuclear distinction works, we can see roughly what the distinction is supposed to be and how it helps with Russell's existent round square problem. It is not the only reply in the literature, however. As we will see in Section 7.2, Deflationary Meinongians also put forth solutions to Russell's problem.

7.2 Deflationary Meinongianism: Some Examples

In this section we're going to explore some different examples of Deflationary Meinongianism. In contrast with the Robust Meinongianism of Section 7.1, on each of these views, the nonexistent objects exemplify a sparse collection of properties. Precisely, which properties they exemplify will differ from view to view.

7.2.1 Zalta

In Zalta (1983, 1988) and Bueno and Zalta (2017), Edward Zalta develops a theory of nonexistent objects. Zalta's nonexistent objects differ from those of the Robust Meinongian in important ways. First, none of them are beyond being. Indeed, Zalta argues that a theory of nonexistent objects has no need for objects that are beyond being (Zalta 1988, pp. 135 ff.). Second, Zalta's nonexistent objects are necessarily nonexistent (Zalta 1988, p. 21). Third, at the core of Zalta's view is a distinction between *encoding* and *exemplifying* a property. Here is Zalta's characterization of the difference between these two different ways of having a property:

> To get an idea of what this distinction amounts to, consider the difference between real and fictional detectives. We can usually talk with, hire, and pay for the services of real detectives. Not so with fictional detectives; they are not the kind of thing we could talk to, or hire, etc. The natural way of explaining this difference is to say that fictional detectives don't have the property of being a detective in quite the same way that real ones do. Real detectives exemplify the property, whereas fictional detectives do not. We shall say that the latter encode the property, however. Things that exemplify the property of being a detective exist, having a location in space and time, are made of flesh and bones, think, solve crimes, and so on, whereas things that just encode the property of being a detective are abstract and do not exemplify any of these characteristics. (Zalta 1988, p. 17)

We can see that many of the properties that a Robust Meinongian will claim are exemplified by nonexistent objects Zalta will say are *encoded* by nonexistent objects. Zalta thinks that with this distinction (which originated in Meinong's pupil Mally and was revived in contemporary times by Rapaport [1978]), he can do much of the work that traditional Meinongian theories can do.

One might wonder to what extent Zalta's theory is truly a Meinongian theory. Zalta's nonexistent objects are abstract and have being, whereas the Robust Meinongian's nonexistent objects are concrete and are beyond being. Indeed, Zalta's view looks somewhat like part of Meinong's own view on which concrete objects exist and abstract objects don't exist though have being. It is also somewhat like Russell's metaphysics in his 1903 *Principles of Mathematics*, on which there are nonexistent objects that nevertheless have being. Robust Meinongians like Dale Jacquette have argued that Zalta's theory isn't truly a Meinongian theory. Jacquette calls Zalta's theory an "intensional theory of quasi-Platonic-Fregean objects" that is "outside the fold of genuine Meinongian referential and predicational semantics" (Jacquette 2015, p. 250).

It is worth noting that Zalta himself (e.g., Bueno and Zalta 2017, pp. 764–5) claims that there are two metaphysics that are compatible with the formalism of his theory. One (his preferred metaphysics) is the metaphysics described previously, on which abstract objects have only being and encode properties, and concrete objects fully exist and don't encode properties. The other is a metaphysics on which abstracta and concrete objects both exist, and abstracta but not concreta encode properties. At some point the question of whether a theory is Meinongian may seem to be merely semantic. But, if we return to our statement of Meinongianism from Chapter 1, we can see that the question of whether Zalta is in our sense a Meinongian or not centers on whether on his view there are nonexistent objects in the scope of our widest quantifiers. On Zalta's preferred rendering of his own view, he is indeed a Meinongian, though of a different sort than the Robust Meinongian.

One question that arises immediately upon considering Zalta's view is this: Which properties do abstracta encode, and which do they exemplify? We aren't given an analysis of encoding versus exemplifying in Zalta. Indeed, encoding a property is a primitive of Zalta's formal theory. But he does have things to say about which properties abstract objects exemplify.

> [A] question arises as to which properties [abstract] objects exemplify. Strictly speaking, the theory doesn't say (other than the property of being non-ordinary). For the most part, we can rely upon our intuitions to say, for example, that they exemplify the negations of ordinary properties, such as being non-round, being non-red, etc. [Abstract] objects also exemplify intentional properties and relations such as being thought about (by so and so), being searched for, etc. These intuitions serve well for most purposes, but there may be occasions where we want to disregard some of them, in return for theoretical benefits. (Zalta 1988, pp. 30–1)

The decision procedure for Zalta here sounds like that from Routley and Parsons as to which properties are nuclear or extranuclear.

Elsewhere, Zalta says,

> Some of us may share the following intuitions. Abstract objects do not exemplify the following properties: being round, having a shape, being red, having a color, being large, having a size, being soft, having a texture, having mass, having spatio-temporal location, being visible, being capable of thought ... being capable of feeling, etc. ... If these intuitions are true ... [abstract] objects exemplify the negations of these properties and relations.

> These properties are "ordinary" properties and relations of existing objects ... They are to be distinguished from ... relations such as being abstract, being thought about, being written about, being worshipped, being more famous than, etc. Note that many of these are "intentional" relations. We can easily imagine that abstract objects exemplify these ... relations. (Zalta 1988, pp. 38–9)

So we're given some guidance as to sorting properties that are exemplified versus those that are encoded, even if we aren't given an analysis of either concept.[4]

Zalta's characterization of the distinction between exemplifying and encoding is open to at least three sorts of criticisms. The first is that Zalta's view is anti-realist in that it leaves whether a property is encoded or exemplified up to human decision-making. For instance, Jacquette says of the passage about real and fictional detectives quoted earlier (Zalta 1988, p. 17):

> This makes the question whether an object encodes or exemplifies a property depend in part on ad hoc decisions taken on a case-by-case basis. However, it is hard to see how such a fundamental semantic distinction could possibly be a matter of decision. Surely abstract objects encode or exemplify properties independently of the contingent existence or nonexistence of decision-makers. This should especially be true in Zalta's ontology, where the existence of any ordinary object, including persons or minds capable of semantic theorizing, is supposed to be logically contingent. (Jacquette 2015, pp. 251–2)

I find this criticism of Zalta a bit strange. Zalta isn't saying that what makes it the case that a property is exemplified (or encoded) is a decision made by humans. Rather, he's saying that although the formal theory doesn't give an answer as to whether a property is exemplified, we can use our intuitions to discern whether a property is exemplified. Even if the formal theory did give an answer, the answer would be tested against the same sorts of intuitions that Zalta has in mind here.

The second criticism of Zalta is that the distinction is either vague or *ad hoc*. We see claims of its vagueness from people like Berto (2012, p. 134 ff.), Berto et al. (2020), and Jacquette (2015). The last, after pointing out that "Zalta's logic deliberately offers no general principle for determining when an abstract object encodes or exemplifies a property," says,

> The indefiniteness and ambiguity that Zalta allows in the application of the dual modes of predication or encoding-exemplification distinction may suggest that Zalta has not so much identified an interesting semantic difference between two ways in which objects have properties, but gerrymanders the stereotopic left-side/right-side predicate syntax more or less arbitrarily to impose order on a set of problems that arise when we attempt to make true predications of nonexistent objects. (Jacquette 2015, p. 253)

It is true that in Zalta, there is no general principle that determines whether a property is exemplified or encoded. But we have an idea of the sorts of properties that are encoded versus those that are exemplified by a nonexistent object, as we saw in the quote from Zalta (1988, pp. 38–9) earlier. There are other debates in metaphysics where we don't have an analysis of competing concepts, but we have a rough idea of how to sort objects as falling under one or the other. For instance, consider the distinction between abstract and concrete objects. Few philosophers, nominalists included, doubt there is a distinction between abstract and concrete objects. Yet, we don't have a good analysis of the difference between the two. One might be tempted to claim that abstracta are acausal and concreta are capable of entering into causal relations. However, this too seems wrong; a symphony may fill me with joy, or the rate of inflation may cause me to pay off a debt (see Friedell 2020 for discussion). In spite of the lack of analysis, I can produce a list of which objects are abstract and which are concrete; this suggests to me that we understand the conceptual distinction even without an analysis. We are in a similar position with Zalta's distinction between exemplifying and encoding. Thus, I don't think that the fact that we don't have an analysis of the difference should put us off Zalta's theory.

There is also the criticism that Zalta's theory is *ad hoc*. Suppose that the distinction were generated wholly for the purposes of avoiding problems of the sort Russell raised for Meinong with existent round squares. Would that be so bad? If the theory is coherent, not open to serious objections, and explains a range of phenomena that need to be explained, then surely Zalta is *prima facie* entitled in accepting theory, whatever its etiology. Zalta is entitled to the theory in the same way I have argued the independence actualist is, or David Lewis (1986, pp. 3–5) argues he is entitled to his theory. All three are entitled to their theory so long as it is coherent and there are no serious objections to it.

There is a third objection to Zalta's encoding–exemplification distinction, and that is linguistic. Consider the following two sentences:

(S1) Holmes is an abstract object.

(S2) Holmes is a detective.

On Zalta's theory, (S1) comes out true only if the relation expressed by the "is" in the sentence involves the *exemplification* relation. (S2) comes out true only if the relation expressed by the "is" in the sentence involves the *encoding* relation. So, the word "is" is ambiguous between these two sentences. We can represent this with the use of subscripts, where "is$_{ex}$" involves the "is" of exemplification and "is$_{en}$" involves the "is" of encoding.

(S1') Holmes is$_{ex}$ an abstract object.

(S1") Holmes is$_{en}$ an abstract object.

(S2') Holmes is$_{ex}$ a detective.

(S2") Holmes is$_{en}$ a detective.

Zalta would say that (S1') and (S2") are true, while (S1") and (S2') are false. If there is this ambiguity in predication, though, it should manifest itself in linguistic analysis of the sentences. There are several standard linguistic tests for ambiguity (see, e.g., Cruse [1997] and Zwicky and Sadock [1975] for discussion).

Cruse (1997) notes that in cases of ambiguity, the meanings of the ambiguous terms stand in antagonistic relations to one another. This can give rise to an almost funny sort of linguistic oddness, *zeugma*, when ambiguous words are referenced together in a sentence. Consider:

(S3) J.P. Morgan and Huck Finn are both at the bank.

(S4) The soap bubble and the waiter are both floating.

In (S3), we have two senses of "bank"—one denoting a place where money is kept and the other denoting a boundary of a river. In (S4), we have two senses of "float"—one involving hovering in mid-air and the other involving being reassigned in one's work to cover an area of need. When we conflate these two senses of each term in the way we have in these two sentences, the result is an infelicity that is almost funny. Compare these sentences to

(S5) Eric [a police detective] and Holmes are both detectives.

With (S5), there is no zeugma. This suggests that there is no ambiguity in the sense of "is" as Zalta's theory would indicate.

As a matter of linguistics, then, there doesn't seem to be the ambiguity in English with "is" that Zalta posits. It would be striking if there were, however. Competent, reflective speakers of modern English and its ancestors do not and have never agreed that there is the ambiguity that Zalta claims there is. One would expect that we would have noticed this ambiguity if it existed in English and other natural languages, in the way that we have noticed the apparent ambiguity between the "is of identity" and the "is of predication."[5]

7.2.2 Crane

Tim Crane (2013) develops a Deflationary Meinongian theory on which nonexistent objects exemplify very few properties. Indeed, apart from *nonexistence*, they exemplify only representation-dependent properties (Crane 2013, p. 68). (Crane calls these "pleonastic" properties, following Schiffer's [2003] usage of the term.) For example, Sherlock Holmes may have properties like *being a fictional detective, being thought of by readers of the Holmes stories*, and *being referred to by philosophers*. Crane argues that the sorts of properties that the Robust Meinongian would claim that nonexistent objects have—for example, *being a detective, being a planet*, or *being a horse*— are existence entailing. For instance, he says of Pegasus,

> Is Pegasus a horse in the same sense that the Darley Arabian is a horse? [H]ere are a few things we actually know about horses: they are normally born from other horses, as a result of mating between a male and female horse. No such thing happened to Pegasus: no act of mating resulted in the birth of Pegasus. (Crane 2013, p. 62)

He continues in this vein about the planet Vulcan, which was thought to orbit between Mercury and the sun:

> Similarly, it is not true that Vulcan is a planet. To be a planet (in the relevant sense) is to orbit the sun (our sun). Yet Vulcan never orbited the sun. If it had, then there would have been nine planets not eight. To orbit the sun, a body must traverse a course through space around the actual body that

is the sun. Vulcan never did this. This is one of the reasons why it is not a planet. (Crane 2013, p. 62)

We will consider these sorts of arguments (which are effectively arguments against Robust Meinongianism) in Section 7.3.1.

7.2.3 Priest

Graham Priest (2005, 2008, 2016) develops a theory on which nonexistent objects exemplify (actually) very few properties.[6] In this the theory looks like that of Crane. But Priest adds an element that Crane's account (explicitly) lacks: Nonexistent objects exemplify a wide range of properties *at other worlds*. Because of the use of possible and impossible worlds in the theory, Priest's view has come to be known as "modal Meinongianism." What sorts of properties do nonexistent objects have actually, according to Priest? He says,

> According to [my view] they have relatively few. They can have intentional properties such as being thought of, or being famous; they can have logical properties, such as being identical to or different from something; they can have status properties, such as being possible or nonexistent. (Priest 2016, p. 216)

Priest's principal reasoning for thinking that objects exemplify few properties is the same as Crane's: Most properties that the Robust Meinongian would say that nonexistent objects have are existence entailing. In particular, any properties that involve causal powers are existence entailing.

One immediate puzzle for Priest's view has to do with the role objects' having properties in other worlds is supposed to play. I have lots of properties in other worlds; for instance, I'm immune to disease, or I can fly, or bullets can't harm me. But my having those properties in other worlds doesn't do anything to help me here in the actual world, α. If I am sick from some disease, it is no comfort to tell me that in other worlds I am immune to all diseases. The fact that I could have been immune to the disease doesn't help me actually here in α. This should lead us to wonder why Priest thinks that nonexistent objects' having properties in other worlds is supposed to improve upon a metaphysics like Crane's.

To address this, it's worth looking at Priest's own words on the issue. After that, we will consider how different conceptions of possible worlds affect how one might answer the question of why Priest's metaphysics is to be preferred over a metaphysics like Crane's.

In a symposium on the first edition of Priest's *Toward Non-Being*, Frederick Kroon argues that Priest should allow that objects actually exemplify a wider range of properties. He says,

> People admire Gandalf, for example, much as they might admire Bill Clinton. But note that people are very clear why they admire Gandalf. They admire him because of such things as his uncompromising goodness. They do not admire him because he is fictionally represented as being of uncompromising goodness, and so has un-compromising goodness in some distant world in which he exists (that might make them admire a certain moral streak in the author, not admire Gandalf himself). (Kroon 2008, p. 201)

For Priest, Gandalf is not uncompromisingly good. He lacks any such property in the actual world.

Priest replies to Kroon,

> People admire Gandalf for the things he does—but these are the things he does in the worlds that realize the story that Tolkien told us. Of course, there are other worlds where Gandalf is not very admirable; where, for example, he sells out the Shire for a kilo of cocaine. It is for his acts in the Tolkien worlds that we admire him. (Priest 2008, p. 217)

But what Kroon says here seems right. Suppose I'm Priest, and I want to say I admire Gandalf, though Gandalf actually has no properties that would make him admirable. I admire him, rather, for properties Gandalf has at other worlds. Surely, the same reasoning would render admirable *anyone* who exists actually. Suppose I notice the look of horror on a colleague's face after I tell her that I admire Donald Trump. I retort, "No, no, no. I don't admire him for the way he *actually* is. Actually he's literally one of the worst people alive. But in other worlds he's a fine fellow indeed. He's humble, respectful, and has dedicated himself to lifting the lot of the poor and downtrodden." Well, that'd be weird. Given what Trump is actually, I don't (and shouldn't) admire him. And I don't admire him any more for being possibly a good person. (Indeed, pick the most loathsome person you wish; there are worlds where that person is supremely virtuous.) The same goes with Gandalf. It is Gandalf's actual properties for which Priest should admire Gandalf, not those he could have had.

To this point we've been operating with a nonspecific conception of what worlds are and what it is to have a property at a world. But it would seem to matter for the modal Meinongian what sorts of things worlds are. Priest (2016, pp. 138 ff.) thinks that his metaphysics is compatible with either a Lewisian (1986) concretist conception of worlds or an abstractionist conception of worlds of the sort that Plantinga (1974) defends. Priest leans in the direction of worlds being concrete and nonexistent, though he thinks that some worlds may need to be abstract (e.g., worlds where nothing exists). The abstract worlds, if any, would be nonexistent as well for Priest; as he thinks abstract objects are nonexistent. It is Priest's contention that we can do much of the work of a traditional Meinongian theory by focusing on properties objects have in other worlds. But whether worlds are abstract or concrete, I think there is a problem for Priest. One might think that when we say that I admire Gandalf, who is uncompromisingly good in other worlds, I'm admiring an uncompromisingly good wizard who is Gandalf. But on either a concretist or an abstractionist conception of worlds, I'm not doing that.

To see this, first suppose worlds are abstract. Priest claims that Gandalf has very few properties actually, though he has many properties in other worlds. But there isn't an object in the scope of our widest quantifiers that has the properties in question (e.g., having uncompromising goodness) that is identical with Gandalf. Rather, what we have are abstract representations (e.g., states of affairs) that there could be such a being. If I admire Gandalf only for his uncompromising goodness in other worlds, I'm not admiring a wizard who is uncompromisingly good. I'm admiring someone who isn't good at all but who could be.

On the other hand, suppose that worlds are concrete. Then there is something in the scope of our widest quantifiers that is a wizard and is uncompromisingly good. But that's not Gandalf. Rather, it's some other being sufficiently like Gandalf to provide for truth conditions for modal Gandalf sentences, or make it the case that Gandalf has certain *de re* modal properties, or both. So either I'm admiring sparsely propertied Gandalf who isn't uncompromisingly good or I'm admiring an uncompromisingly good wizard who isn't Gandalf.

So I think we can see, especially once we consider different possibilities as to the nature of worlds, that objects' having properties in other worlds isn't doing the metaphysical work Priest thinks it is.

7.3 Robust and Deflationary Meinongianism

To this point, we have set out some different versions of Robust and Deflationary Meinongianism. We turn now to the question of which of the two general sorts of Meinongian one should be, if one is to be a Meinongian. We will begin with arguments for Deflationary over Robust Meinongianism. We will then consider reasons why one might be a Robust, rather than a Deflationary, Meinongian.

7.3.1 Reasons to Prefer Deflationary Meinongianism to Robust Meinongianism

7.3.1.1 The Argument from Empirically Manifest Properties

Why might someone plump for some sort of Deflationary Meinongianism over any sort of Robust Meinongianism? The principal arguments for Deflationary Meinongianism take the form of arguments against Robust Meinongianism, alongside a perhaps tacit assumption that we should be Meinongians of some sort. Thus, in this section we will consider arguments against Robust Meinongianism, as they are made by defenders of Deflationary Meinongianism.

There are two sorts of arguments against Robust Meinongianism that one sees in the Meinongian literature. We will call the first *the argument from empirically manifest properties*. This argument trades on the fact that if nonexistent objects had the sorts of properties that ordinary existing objects did, we'd be aware of the nonexistent objects. We could think of Russell's existing golden mountain objection as an instance of the argument from empirically manifest properties. Russell supposes that for Meinong there has to be an object that satisfies every meaningful definite description; and thus there is an existing golden mountain. But we know there is no existing golden mountain, as we've never found one. We'd notice it if it existed![7]

Here are two contemporary examples of this sort of argument, from Berto and Priest, and Anthony Everett, respectively:

> Now, we ask [Robust Meinongians]: how could Holmes literally possess those features [like being a detective or living in 221b Baker Street]? In

reality, Baker Street 221b hosted an enterprise, the Abbey Road Building Society, and it has never been the house of any private detective. It is literally false, not true, that 221b is, or has ever been, Holmes' home. In one of the Doyle stories we are told that Holmes has tea with William Gladstone ... How can this be literally true? William Gladstone is a real (past) existent, who certainly never had tea with any purely fictional object. (Berto and Priest 2014, p. 188)

If I write a story in which Anna Karenina is currently sitting in my chair, she is surely not currently occupying that chair the way I am. And suppose I write a story in which a little green man is sitting on your desk shouting loudly, pulling faces at you, and trying to attract your attention. This surely does not mean something is sitting on your desk shouting loudly, pulling faces at you, and trying to attract your attention. (Everett 2013, p. 169)[8]

What should the Robust Meinongian say about the argument from empirically manifest properties? The standard reply to this sort of argument has been to invoke the nuclear–extranuclear distinction. Consider the existing golden mountain case: We then say that the nonexistent object in question exemplifies the nuclear properties *being golden* and *being a mountain* and doesn't exemplify the extranuclear property *existence*. But we can quickly see that the nuclear–extranuclear distinction won't help with many cases where we would expect the nonexistent object to have properties the having of which we would observe. Suppose, as the Robust Meinongian would like to say, that nonexistent Holmes exemplifies properties like *having a body*, *being spatial*, and *having mass*. Suppose we add that he exemplifies *living in 221b Baker Street*. Then why haven't the inhabitants of 221b Baker Street encountered him? We can see that all these properties are nuclear properties, so we aren't able to say that nonexistent Holmes doesn't thereby exemplify some of them in virtue of their being extranuclear. Indeed, this is how it should be for the Robust Meinongian; the Robust Meinongian holds that nonexistent Holmes does exemplify these sorts of properties.

If the nuclear–extranuclear distinction won't help the Robust Meinongian across the board with the argument from empirically manifest properties, what should the Robust Meinongian say in reply to this sort of argument? To try to answer this, it's worth noting the features of the Holmes case that generate the problem for the Robust Meinongian. It is the conjunction having a body, being spatial, and having mass; with living in 221b Baker Street, that led to the question of why the inhabitants of 221b haven't encountered him. In particular, the problem with empirically manifest properties is generated when there is an overlap of the nonexistent and existent worlds. In this case, the overlap is in 221b Baker Street in London.

Some have thought that names of existing things (e.g., "221b Baker Street" or "London") when used in fiction denote existing objects (e.g., Kripke 2013, pp. 74–5; Parsons 1980, p. 51). But here's an argument that if names of existing things (e.g., "London") refer when used in a fictional context (as the Robust Meinongian thinks), the name changes reference. When he writes his stories, Doyle is able to make London be anything he wants it to be. It can be clean or dirty, full of pubs or devoid of them. But Doyle has no such power over existent, concrete London. Therefore, if "London" refers in a fictional context it doesn't refer to existent, concrete London.

Furthermore, it would seem apart from this last argument that the Robust Meinongian is *prima facie* warranted in saying that names used in fiction change denotation. The Robust Meinongian theory is that nonexistent objects, like Sherlock Holmes, exemplify the same sorts of properties that ordinary existing objects do. Holmes exemplifies properties like *being a detective*, *wearing a deerstalker hat*, and *living in 221b Baker Street*. If the evidence of our senses is that there isn't such a person living in the flat referred to with "221b Baker Street, London" in nonfictional contexts, then the Robust Meinongian is warranted in positing that "221b Baker Street" when used in fictional contexts changes reference. There's nothing in the Robust Meinongian theory *per se* to saddle her with the view that nonexistent objects must inhabit existing places. If we have empirical justification that there aren't any such objects in existing places, then the Robust Meinongian simply ought to deny that, for example, Sherlock Holmes lives in the flat referred to with "221b Baker Street, London" in nonfictional contexts.

What sort of thing does "221b Baker Street" refer to for the Robust Meinongian, if it's not the existing flat? We may look to the descriptions given in the Doyle stories: It contains a couch, a fireplace, some chairs, curtains, and sometimes people like Holmes and Watson. That is, it's a nonexistent flat with the attributes spelled out by Doyle in the Holmes stories.

There are options for the Robust Meinongian at this point. Is the flat complete such that it exemplifies every property or its complement? Or is it incomplete in the manner that Parsons and Routley think about some nonexistent objects? Is the flat located in nonexistent space? One might be tempted to say that it does exemplify every property or its complement, as it is a necessary truth that every object exemplifies every property or its complement. One might also be tempted to say that the flat is located in nonexistent space, as it is a necessary truth that every flat—or anything with a couch and a fireplace—is located in space.[9] But perhaps such necessary truths apply only to existing objects. Perhaps, for example, a nonexistent flat can be nonspatial.

One's answers to these questions may be influenced by how realist one is about nonexistent fictional objects. Suppose we think of Doyle, in writing the Holmes stories, as picking out "already-there" nonexistent objects and using them in the course of telling the stories. Then we might be drawn to a view on which the flat does exemplify every property or its complement, even if we are not sure in many cases which it exemplifies. We also might think of Doyle as having picked out an already-there nonexistent city in which the flat is located in nonexistent space. Or, the Robust Meinongian might think that Doyle creates the nonexistent flat when he pens the Holmes stories. In such a case, one might be tempted to say that with some properties, the flat may lack it and its complement.

Some of this might seem metaphysically extravagant. But once one has nonexistent people and flats, how is it any more extravagant to have them in nonexistent spaces and cities? Furthermore, the same reasoning by which one arrives at a nonexistent Holmes with an abundant array of properties *mutatis mutandis* applies to other things mentioned in the Holmes stories. At any rate, I think the Robust Meinongian has options here. I'm not aware of any arguments that would compel the Robust Meinongian in one direction or another.

These current explorations came about in the context of replying to the argument from empirically manifest properties. In response to it, we said that the Robust Meinongian should plump for the view that objects referred to in fiction are (at least usually) distinct from ordinary existing objects. This holds even when they share a name and many characteristics. Thus, there won't be overlap in these cases between existent and nonexistent objects. But are there ever cases where there is overlap between the existent and the nonexistent? Perhaps there is. As we noted earlier in this book, Mark Hinchliff (1988) has defended the view that nonexistent past events may play a role in grounding past truths and cross-time relations. But central to our purposes here is that the Robust Meinongian has a reply to the argument from empirically manifest properties.

7.3.1.2 The Argument from the Existence Entailment of Properties

We will call the second principal argument against Robust Meinongianism *the argument from the existence entailment of properties*. According to this argument, properties that the Robust Meinongian claims that nonexistent objects have are necessarily such that anything that has them exists. Sometimes the entailment is immediately from the property in question, or sometimes having the property in question entails that the individual has some other property, and the having of the other property entails *existence*. Here is a particularly vivid statement of this sort of argument from Graham Priest:

> As a non-existent, Holmes cannot literally have features that entail existence, like living in a real street, having tea with Gladstone, or being a detective. If something is a detective and lives on a London street, then, it is natural to think, it is a human being, a physical object, a spatiotemporal occupier, and endowed with causal properties. One might ask where the person is, or why, as a detective, they cannot help the metropolitan police to solve crimes. Answer: things lacking real existence are not anywhere, and cannot have such existence-entailing properties. (Priest 2016, p. 221)

Tim Crane gives an argument of a similar flavor:

> Objects have natures. What their natures are is a matter of empirical or metaphysical study. But having some of these natures requires that those objects exist. It is in the nature of horses, planets, golden things, living things (and so on) to exist. Non-existent things do not have what it takes to have the properties of these things. Non-existent objects cannot have properties like being a horse, being golden, being a detective, and nor can they stand in relations like killing. (Crane 2013, p. 63)

There is a lot to unpack in these arguments. Some of what we will have to say about them will relate to what we noted in our discussion of the argument from empirically manifest properties in Section 7.3.1.1. Let's begin with Priest's argument. He begins by listing some existing-entailing attributes: *living in a real street*, *having tea with Gladstone*, and *being a detective*. Why are these existence entailing? If we parse living on a real street as living on an existing street, then perhaps we can see why Holmes would need to be existent to do that. The same goes with having tea with Gladstone: If the name here denotes the existing person Gladstone, then we also can see perhaps why Holmes would need to be existent to do this. However, as we saw in Section 7.3.1.1, the Robust Meinongian need not attribute these sorts of properties to nonexistent Holmes. She may claim that nonexistent Holmes lives on a concrete, nonexistent (and real!) street. And while Holmes doesn't have tea with the existing Gladstone, he does have tea with a nonexistent concrete individual who is enough like Gladstone (including being called "Gladstone") to serve the purposes of the story being told. We aren't given any argument from Priest that only existing things can exemplify *being a detective*.

Priest continues,

> If something is a detective and lives on a London street, then, it is natural to think, it is a human being, a physical object, a spatiotemporal occupier, and endowed with causal properties. (Priest 2016, p. 221)

The only problem here for the Robust Meinongian is the claim that Holmes lives on the streets of the existing city London. But, as we've seen, the Robust Meinongian has reason to claim that proper names in fiction change denotation such that the city denoted by Doyle in the Holmes story when he uses the name "London" isn't concrete, existing London.

Priest's argument finishes with the following:

> One might ask where the person is, or why, as a detective, they cannot help the metropolitan police to solve crimes. Answer: things lacking real existence are not anywhere, and cannot have such existence-entailing properties. (Priest 2016, p. 221)

I think now we can see what the Robust Meinongian should say here. Holmes is a nonexistent object who is a detective who helps a nonexistent police department (named "the Metropolitan Police") to solve crimes. We know that he doesn't help the existing metropolitan police, however. (How? We can ask them.) The Robust Meinongian can say that Holmes is somewhere: on a nonexistent street, in a nonexistent flat.

We can see that the Crane argument is not much beyond an assertion of the falsity of Robust Meinongianism. It is precisely the view of the Robust Meinongian that nonexistent objects can have natures and exemplify properties like *being a horse*, *being golden*, and *being a detective*.

I think the Crane argument is dialectically instructive, however. It is very difficult for me to see how a non-question-begging argument from existence entailment of properties would go. It is the view of the Robust Meinongian that nonexistent objects can have the sorts of properties that ordinary existing objects do. There's nothing obvious about these particular properties over and against other properties that suggest that a nonexistent object can't have the particular property, unless the property involves reference to a particular existing individual (e.g., *having tea with Gladstone*). At most the objector can point to other properties that the nonexistent object would have to have to have the property in question. At that point the Robust Meinongian may maintain that the nonexistent object in question has those as well (or a suitable substitute if the properties in question involve directly existing individuals); or doesn't need to have the properties, as the necessary property entailment holds only with properties of existing individuals. Maybe the objector like Crane is right in asserting that many of the sorts of properties the Robust Meinongian thinks nonexistent objects exemplify are existence entailing. But it's very tough to see how to generate a cogent argument for this claim that doesn't beg the question against the Robust Meinongian.

7.3.2 Reasons to Prefer Robust Meinongianism to Deflationary Meinongianism

Thus, I don't think that there are compelling reasons for the Meinongian to reject Robust Meinongianism. What sorts of considerations are there *in favor* of Robust Meinongianism? As I see it, the main arguments in favor of Robust Meinongianism over Deflationary Meinongianism come from the initial motivations for Meinongianism that we discussed in Chapter 4. There we noted that there are typically three reasons given for being a Meinongian: proper treatment of intentional verbs, negative existentials, and fictional discourse.

Let's start with the first, proper treatment of intentional verbs. The Robust Meinongian is able to say that the object that Albertus Magnus seeks exemplifies *being an object that turns lead into gold*. That is, he's really searching for an object that exemplifies the properties that the Philosopher's Stone is said to have. According to the Deflationary Meinongian, this is false. Nonexistent objects don't exemplify properties like *being an object that turns lead into gold*. As we saw in our discussion of different versions of Deflationary Meinongianism, there are things that the Deflationary Meinongian can say to ease the sting of this consequence. Zalta will say that Magnus searches for an object that *encodes* the property *being an object that turns lead into gold*. For Zalta, then, the Philosopher's Stone *almost-is* or *kind-of is* an object that turns lead into gold. Priest will say that Magnus searches for an object that exemplifies *being an object that turns lead into gold* in other worlds. But no Deflationary Meinongian is able to say that Magnus searches for an object that is (in our ordinary sense of predication) something that turns lead into gold. If you were to ask Magnus what the object he's searching for is like, he'd reply with a list of properties that the Deflationary Meinongian would deny that any nonexistent object can have.

The objection to Deflationary Meinongianism here is similar to a well-known objection to views on which what Magnus searches for is an abstract object. On Roderick Chisholm's (1986) treatment of intentional verbs, Magnus searches for a property, something like *being the only location of the object that turns lead into gold*. Why didn't Chisholm have the search be for the haecceity of the Philosopher's Stone, *being the Philosopher's Stone*? My suspicion is that he sees that it is open to the objection that what Magnus is searching for is the Stone itself rather than the essence of the Stone. Rather, Chisholm would have Magnus search for a property that picks out a place where the Stone is located. However, the basic structure of the objection remains; on Chisholm's view Magnus searches for an abstract object. Tomberlin and McGuinness note this about a Chisholmian explanation of Ponce De Leon's search for the Fountain of Youth:

> It seems hardly credible that [sentences about someone searching for a nonexistent object] are properly explicated in terms of a person's pursuit of an attribute. If asked, we think, Ponce de Leon quite properly would have resisted the suggestion that the object of his search was abstract rather than

concrete. His folly was to believe that there was actually a fountain of youth to be found. (Tomberlin and McGuinness 1994, p. 463)

The problem, then, is that Chisholm is not able to say that the object that Magnus searches for has the sorts of properties Magnus thinks it does. The Deflationary Meinongian has the same problem. The nonexistent object that Magnus searches for isn't at all like what Magnus believes it to be. Perhaps it is represented as being that way (Crane, Zalta), or is sort-of that way (Zalta), or could be that way (Priest). But the Deflationary Meinongian has to deny that the nonexistent objects that are the objects of attitudes are like what they are believed to be like.

The Deflationary Meinongian fares better when it comes to negative existential sentences. If we return to the Anubis case from Chapter 4, there is a nonexistent object—Anubis—to serve as the content of the name "Anubis" in the sentence "Anubis does not exist." Thus, the sentence can express a complete proposition. The Deflationary Meinongian is able to say that when one utters "Anubis does not exist," she is truly denying existence of an object.

To see how the Deflationary Meinongian deals with discourse around fictional characters, consider first a problem for views of fictional characters on which they are actually existing abstract objects (e.g., Salmon 1998; Thomasson 1998; van Inwagen 1977). If Sherlock Holmes is an abstract object, then many of the claims made of Sherlock Holmes in the stories are literally false. Thus, Sherlock Holmes doesn't exemplify properties like *being a detective* or *wearing a deerstalker hat*; no abstract object exemplifies those properties. The Robust Meinongian about fictional characters, on the other hand, is able to maintain that Holmes does exemplify properties like *being a detective* and *wearing a deerstalker hat*. The Deflationary Meinongian has problems with fictional characters that are analogous to those had by the abstract object theorist about fictional characters. For the Deflationary Meinongian, it won't be true that Holmes exemplifies properties like *being a detective* or *wearing a deerstalker hat*. The Deflationary Meinongian may say that Holmes could exemplify these properties (Priest), or sort-of exemplifies these properties (Zalta), or is represented as exemplifying these properties (Crane, Zalta). But, given an ordinary referential semantics, sentences like "Holmes is a detective" strictly are false on the Deflationary Meinongian metaphysic.

One might have thought that if one were going to admit nonexistent objects into one's ontology, one would allow them to have the sorts of properties needed for many intentional and fictional claims about them to come out true on a straightforward reading of the claims. But the Deflationary Meinongian doesn't do this. The ability for the Robust Meinongian to account for the truth of these claims is the strongest consideration in its favor over and against Deflationary Meinongianism. Indeed, it's not clear to me why one would be a Meinongian at that point, rather than an actualist of some sort. If the Meinongian ontology isn't allowing for the truth of fictional or intentional statements, why hold onto the nonexistent objects?

Perhaps not all Deflationary theories are on an equal footing here, though. Because the Philosopher's Stone encodes properties like *being an object that turns lead into gold*, Zalta is able to say that *in some sense*, Magnus is searching for an object that has the properties he thinks it does. Similarly, because Holmes encodes *being a detective*, it is *in some sense* true that Holmes is a detective, and so on. Neither Priest nor Crane avails himself of encoding, and as a result neither is able to make these sorts of claims.

7.4 Robust over Deflationary Meinongianism

In Section 7.3 we saw that the two principal arguments for preferring Deflationary Meinongianism to Robust Meinongianism don't give the Meinongian a compelling case for adopting Deflationary Meinongianism. We also saw that the motivations for being a Meinongian *simpliciter* favor Robust over Deflationary Meinongianism. These factors may be conjoined with the fact that there are problems with two of the best-known sorts of Deflationary views: Zalta's encoding view and modal Meinongianism. Thus, I say to the Meinongian unconvinced by the arguments in favor of independence actualism in the first six chapters of this book: Adopt some version of Robust Meinongianism. If one is going to accept nonexistent objects into one's ontology, they ought to do the metaphysical work that led one to Meinongianism in the first place.

8

God and Necessary Existence

In this chapter I want to examine the claim that God is responsible for the existence and natures of necessarily existing abstracta. Many theists throughout history have thought this claim to be true. But does it make sense? How can necessary existents depend on anything? In the first section, we'll begin by examining more closely what we're after when we ask about the relationship between God and necessarily existing things. In the second section, we will turn to some motivations that have led some to claim that necessary existents depend on God. In the third and fourth sections, we will examine some different views about the relationship between God and necessarily existing abstracta. In the last section, we will take stock of the analyses of different positions in the chapter.

8.1 Clarifying the Issue

The main question we will address in this chapter is this: Does God ground the existence of necessarily existing abstract objects? It is perhaps a more general question than a question one might at first ask: Did God create necessarily existing abstracta? But it is the main question that philosophers who have written about the relation between God and abstract objects have sought to answer.

Over the past two decades, philosophers have done a great deal of work on the notion of grounding (see, e.g., Audi 2012; Fine 2001; Koslicki 2012; Rosen 2010; Schaffer 2009). It is thought by many currently working on issues in the metaphysics of grounding that grounding is a primitive, *sui generis* relation. In particular, it is not to be understood as a supervenience or causal relation. How are we then to understand what it is? Philosophers point to particular cases where it is thought to be instanced: Dispositional properties are grounded in categorical properties, the mental is grounded in the physical, the semantic is grounded in the non-semantic, features like smiles or surfaces are grounded in facts about bodies, and so on. To this point, one might think that grounding talk can be captured by our ordinary notion of supervenience. But Fine (2001) claims that Socrates' singleton set is grounded in Socrates, yet, necessarily one exists just if the other does. Thus, it is said, our ordinary modal notion of supervenience won't capture this case of grounding. If we assume (as many in the grounding literature do) that the other cases of grounding are of the same sort as the Socrates-singleton case is, then our ordinary notion of supervenience won't capture them either.

Our discussion of the question of God's grounding the existence of necessarily existing abstracta bears on the general conversation about the nature of grounding. First, we can note that our divine grounding case stands alongside the Socrates-singleton case in showing that ordinary supervenience won't capture the grounding relationship properly. For instance, suppose we say that God grounds the existence of the number two. And suppose we follow the consensus of theists over time in thinking God is a necessary being. We can then note that, necessarily, God exists just if two does. According to ordinary notions of supervenience, the number two supervenes on God, and conversely. But we are to think that God grounds the existence of two, and not vice versa. Second, we have here in the case of divine grounding of abstracta a case where the grounding relationship is typically spelled out in other, familiar terms (and thus isn't *sui generis*). As we will see, a number of different philosophers who think that God grounds the existence of necessarily existing abstract objects think that God does so in a causal manner. Others think that the grounding takes place in that necessarily existing abstracta are identical with divine mental states.

One might look at those who claim that God causes necessarily existing abstract objects or that they are identical with divine mental states as not asserting that God grounds the existence of necessarily existing abstracta. But as we will see, each of these sorts of theorists really *is* saying that God grounds the existence of necessarily existing abstract objects. Thus, it might be better to cast our lot with those who are skeptical that there is a *sui generis* grounding relationship that metaphysicians investigate. Or, if there is such a relationship in some cases of grounding, it isn't present in all cases of grounding (it isn't "univocal"—see Hofweber [2009] and Daly [2012] for discussion). After all, it is perfectly sensible to recast "Do necessarily existing abstract objects depend on God?" as "Are necessarily existing abstract objects grounded in God?"

However we think of the dependence relationship between God and necessarily existing abstract objects, we will want to insist that God is somehow more fundamental than necessarily existing abstract objects. Fundamentality is an asymmetric relationship. Thus, we will construe those who think that God grounds the existence of necessarily existing abstracta as claiming that God is more fundamental than necessarily existing abstracta, and not conversely.

8.2 Motivations for Thinking God Grounds the Existence and Nature of Necessarily Existing Abstract Objects

There are at least two sorts of reasons why someone might be inclined to think that God grounds the existence of necessarily existing abstract objects. The first sort of reason involves central religious texts in monotheistic faiths like Judaism, Christianity, and Islam. Roughly, this sort of reason consists in these texts' assertions or suggestions that God has created everything. If God created everything, it must be that God has created necessarily existing abstract objects as well. Thus, God grounds the existence of these abstract objects. For instance, there are statements in the Hebrew Bible such as Psalm 89:11: "The heavens are yours, the earth also is yours; the world and all that is in it—you have founded them."[1]

Also in the Hebrew Bible is Nehemiah 9:6:

> And Ezra said: "You are the Lord, you alone; you have made heaven, the heaven of heavens, with all their host, the earth and all that is on it, the seas and all that is in them. To all of them you give life, and the host of heaven worships you."

In the New Testament, there are passages like John 1:1–1:4:

> In the beginning was the Word [Logos], and the Word was with God, and the Word was God. He was in the beginning with God. All things came into being through him, and without him not one thing came into being. [The Word to which John refers is Jesus of Nazareth.]

Paul states in Colossians 1:15–16:

> He [Jesus] is the image of the invisible God, the firstborn of all creation; for in him all things in heaven and on earth were created, things visible and invisible, whether thrones or dominions or rulers or powers—all things have been created through him and for him.

One of the most important documents for Christian faith outside the Hebrew Bible and New Testament, the Nicene Creed of 325, says, "We believe in one God, the Father almighty, maker of all things visible and invisible." The Niceno-Constantinopolitan Creed of 381, a modification of the older Nicene Creed of 325 that is used by the Western Church, begins similarly, "We believe in one God, the Father almighty, maker of heaven and earth, of all things that are visible and invisible."

We see similar sort of claims in Islamic thinking. According to the Qur'an [151], "God is the Creator of all things; He has charge of everything; the keys of the heavens and earth are His" (39:62–63). The Qur'an also says, "This is God, your Lord, there is no God but Him, the Creator of all things, so worship Him; He is in charge of everything" (6:102).

These reasons from authoritative religious texts may not be taken to be conclusive, however. One may take these sorts of texts seriously as an adherent to faiths they define and still hold that God doesn't have creative control over necessarily existing abstract objects. For instance, Peter van Inwagen (2009) argues that the universal quantifier in claims like that of the Nicene Creed's "maker of all things visible and invisible" is implicitly restricted to include only those things that are capable of being created. Necessarily existing abstract objects cannot enter into causal relations, says Van Inwagen, and thus can't be created.[2] But it is worth noting that philosophers who think that if there are necessarily existing abstract objects, God must have some sort of control over them (e.g., Craig 2016) point to texts like those cited previously for justification for this view.

There is a second sort of reasoning that may lead someone to think that God grounds the existence of necessarily existing abstract objects. That is by way of perfect being theology (see Morris [1987, 1989] and Nagasawa [2017] for discussion). Perfect being theology is a way of theorizing *a priori* about God that goes back at least to Anselm of Canterbury. One begins with the claim that God is the greatest possible being, and from there one can derive attributes that

God must have. This method is one way of arriving at God's being omnipotent, omniscient, and perfectly good. Anselm himself famously thought that via perfect being theology, he could conclude that God existed. For our purposes here, we are to imagine two conceptually possible beings: One being grounds or explains the existence of necessarily existing abstract objects, and the other doesn't. We are to see that the being that grounds these abstracta is greater than one who doesn't, and thus we are to conclude that God (the greatest possible being) grounds necessarily existing abstract objects. Sometimes the intuition that the former being is greater than the latter is put in terms of God's aseity, or independence from all other entities. A being with maximal aseity is greater than one without it (other things being equal); and if necessarily existing abstract objects don't depend on God, God lacks maximal aseity.

There likely would be little objection to reasoning to divine grounding of necessarily existing abstracta in the above way, *if it were thought that God could have control over these sorts of abstracta*. However, someone might concur with van Inwagen that abstracta can't enter into causal relations, and say that the only way that abstracta might be grounded in God is via causation. Or someone might think that the idea of a necessarily existing object depending on *anything* is incoherent.[3] If one took either of these positions, one would deny that the being who grounds necessarily existing abstract objects was greater than the one who didn't. (Just as she would deny that a being who can make a square circle is greater than one who can't—there can't be a being who can make a square circle.)

We have noted two sorts of reasons why a theist might think that God grounds the existence of necessarily existing abstract objects. We turn to a discussion of some different answers to our central question: Does God ground the existence of necessarily existing abstract objects? We will consider the merits of a number of different sorts of views that bear on answering this question.

8.3 Four Views on Which All Necessarily Existing Abstracta Are Grounded in God

8.3.1 Theistic Voluntarism

Theistic Voluntarism: Necessarily existing abstracta are caused to exist by God's will or some other normally contingent divine faculty. (Example: Descartes.)

According to the theistic voluntarist, necessarily existing abstract objects depend on the divine will or some other contingent feature of God. This is famously the view of Descartes. In a letter to Mersenne (May 27, 1630), Descartes says,

> You ask me by what kind of causality God established the eternal truths. I reply: by the same kind of causality as he created all things, that is to say, as their efficient and total cause. For it is certain that he is the author of the essence of created things no less than of their existence; and this essence is nothing other than the eternal truths. I do not conceive them as emanating from God like rays from the sun; but I know that God is the author of everything and that these truths are something and consequently that he is their author. (Descartes 1991, p. 25)

Descartes makes the same sorts of claims in his public writings as well (e.g., in the reply to the Sixth Set of Objections [also from Mersenne]). This view seems to take seriously that God truly is maximally powerful; he even has volitional control over things like numbers, properties, and states of affairs. Indeed, even more than with views like theistic emanationism is God in control of abstracta on this view. According to the theistic voluntarist, God could have made different—or no—abstracta like propositions, properties, and states of affairs. God is in control of abstracta like God is in control of any other object: Their existence is subject to God's will.

Of course, the seriousness with which the theistic voluntarist takes divine aseity and sovereignty is also a source of problems for the view. If God could have failed to make the number two, in what sense is the number two a necessary being? One might try to weaken the voluntarist view by claiming that the number two is only weakly necessary: God had to create it, but it is possibly ... possible that it does not exist. However, all worlds that are accessible to the actual world have the number two existing in them. Some of these worlds, though, have a somewhat different divine will relative to the existence of the number two (maybe God somewhat reluctantly wills the existence of the number two in them). And possible relative to those sorts of worlds (or relative to worlds possible to those worlds, etc.) are worlds in which God doesn't will that the number two exist. The key here is that the claim *Necessarily, the number two exists* comes out true on this picture; the number two exists in every possible world relative to the world of evaluation (the actual world). But there are possibly possible worlds in which God doesn't will the existence of the number two. The voluntarist can say that abstracta depend on the will of God and yet really do exist necessarily (just don't say in every possible world, *full stop* [see Plantinga 1980, pp. 95 ff. for further discussion]).

This suggestion risks two sorts of problems. The first is that it doesn't take divine sovereignty seriously enough. Imagine a being who could—in a world possible relative to the actual world—make it the case that the number two doesn't exist. That being might be thought to be more powerful than a being that only possibly possibly could do this. Descartes (in places, at least) seems to have this intuition and thus plumps for a God who could make it the case that the number two didn't exist.

The second concern is that it abandons S5-type modal logic, in which anything that is necessary is necessarily necessary. This is thought by many to be the appropriate system of modal logic to describe the way actual modality is.[4] So there are concerns from both sides for this reply to the objection to voluntarism. On the one hand, it might be thought not to take divine power seriously enough. On the other, it might not make abstracta "necessary enough."

One reason why Descartes is famous for holding to theistic voluntarism is because so few others in the history of theological thought hold to it. And perhaps the main reason why no one else holds to it is because many judge that the theistic voluntarist isn't able to account for the absolute necessity of necessarily existing abstracta. These are objects that if they exist should exist in every possible world, full stop; and once one allows for that, it makes it very difficult to see how it could be up to God's will that these exist. Rather, if they are up to God one winds up with a view like theistic emanationism. We turn to it.

8.3.2 Theistic Emanationism

Theistic Emanationism: Necessarily existing abstracta are caused to exist by some noncontingent divine faculty (e.g., divine cognition). (Examples: Leibniz; Morris and Menzel 1986.)

According to the theistic emanationist, necessarily existing abstract objects are caused to exist by some noncontingent feature of divine activity. The standard feature the emanationist appeals to is divine cognitive activity of some sort. So, the theistic emanationist will say something like that the number two exists because of God's cognitive activity. She will go on to say (and this is how the view is distinct from a theistic voluntarist view) it is not possible (it's true in no possible world, full stop) for God's cognitive activity in this respect to be other than it is. Thus, the theistic emanationist can hold that abstracta really exist in every possible world, full stop (allowing that God does, too).

One example of a theistic emanationist is Leibniz. In his *Monadology* he says,

> 43. It is also true that God is not only the source of existences but also that of essences insofar as they are real, that is, the source of that which is real in possibility. This is because God's understanding is the realm of eternal truths, or that of the ideas on which they depend; without him there would be nothing real in possibles, and not only would nothing exist, but also nothing would be possible.
>
> 44. For if there is a reality in essences or possibilities, or indeed in eternal truths, this reality must be grounded in something existent and actual, and consequently, it must be grounded in the existence of the necessary being, in whom essence involves existence, that is, in whom possible being is sufficient for actual being. (Leibniz 1989, p. 218)

Here Leibniz seems to suggest that necessarily existing abstracta are grounded in divine cognitive activity. It's not clear exactly how to characterize the relation between the cognitive activity and the existence of the abstract objects, but saying that the former causes the latter to exist seems appropriate given his language.

Thomas Morris and Christopher Menzel (1986) also are theistic emanationists. They invoke explicitly causal language in setting out their view, which they call "theistic activism."

> So our suggestion is that the platonistic framework of reality arises out of a creatively efficacious intellective activity of God. It is in this sense that God is the creator of the framework. It depends on him. (Morris and Menzel 1986, p. 356)

They continue later:

> Let us refer to this view, the view that a divine intellectual activity is responsible for the framework of reality, as "theistic activism." A theistic

activist will hold God creatively responsible for the entire modal economy, for what is possible as well as what is necessary and what is impossible. The whole Platonic realm is thus seen as deriving from God. (Morris and Menzel 1986, p. 356)

And on the next page:

God's creation of the framework of reality ... is an activity which is conscious, intentional, and neither constrained nor compelled by anything independent of God and his causally efficacious power. (Morris and Menzel 1986, p. 357)

Theistic emanationism allows the theist to take seriously the claims of religious documents that God creates everything (indeed, the name of Morris and Menzel's paper is "Absolute Creation"), and it avoids the problems that beset theistic voluntarism.

Theistic emanationism then has virtues. However, it has problems of its own. First, some philosophers claim that God already has to have critical properties to be able to cause abstracta to exist. The theistic emanationist claims that God causes properties such as *being omniscient*, *being omnipotent*, *existing necessarily*, *being able to cause abstracta to exist*, and *having cognitive activity to exist*. She also claims that God causes his own haecceity, *being God*, to exist. However, to claim this is to get the dependence relationship backward, one might charge. Surely, God's being able to cause abstract objects to exist must be posterior to his having properties like the ones mentioned earlier. And if God has these properties, they must exist. But, the proponent of this theory is committed to the existence of properties being posterior to God's causing them to exist. Thus, the objection concludes, theistic emanationism is false (see Bergmann and Brower 2006; Davidson 1999; Davison 1991; Leftow 1990a, for discussion of this sort of objection).

This sort of argument has seemed to many to be decisive. However, there is a response that the theistic emanationist can give at this point. It might be claimed that although God's ability to cause abstracta to exist is logically dependent on his having certain properties, it is not causally dependent. The account would be problematically circular only if God's ability to cause abstracta to exist were causally dependent on his having certain properties and his having these properties were, in turn, causally dependent on his having caused these properties to exist. There is a circle of logical dependence here (as there is between any two necessary truths), but there is no circle of causal dependence (see Morris and Menzel 1986 for this sort of reply).

The opponent of theistic emanationism might make the following retort. Certainly, the above response is right in that if there is a problem of circularity, it is one of causal circularity. Earlier, we saw that there for the theistic emanationist is a one-way causal relationship between God's cognitive activity and the existence of abstracta such as *being the number two*. We can say that the necessary existence of *being the number two* (or any abstract object) causally depends on God's having the cognitive activity that he does. Or, perhaps we might say that the necessary existence of *being the number two* causally depends on God's being omniscient, omnipotent, and existing necessarily. However, the entities on which *being the number two* causally depends are themselves properties. On what do they causally depend? It seems that on the emanationist account, they wind up causally depending on themselves. But this is incoherent, one might charge.

Even if the emanationist successfully replies to this first problem for the view, there is a second, and perhaps more serious, objection to the view. We will call this objection "the bootstrapping objection" (see Bergmann and Brower 2006; Davidson 1999; Gould 2014; Leftow 1990a, for discussion of this sort of objection). We can put the concern this way (following Davidson 1999). To cause something to exist is to cause its essence (or, in the terminology of Plantinga 1980, its *nature*) to be exemplified. Suppose God creates a certain table that has as a part of its essence *being red* (we could also pick *being made of wood*). Then God causes the property *being red* to be exemplified by the table when he creates it. Consider the property *being omnipotent*. The property *being exemplified by God* is contained in its essence. So, God causes the property *being exemplified by God* to be exemplified by *being omnipotent* in causing *being omnipotent* to exist. Similar to the manner with which God causes *being red* to be exemplified by the table in exemplifying the table's essence, God causes *being omnipotent* to be exemplified by himself. But surely, God can't cause the property *being omnipotent* to be exemplified by himself: How can God make himself omnipotent? Furthermore, one might think that God's omnipotence should be causally prior to his causing properties to exist. However, on this occasion it is not. Then, if one does think that God's omnipotence should be causally prior to his causing properties to exist, this would be an instance of causal circularity. This sort of argument will work for other properties like *being omniscient* or *having divine cognitive activity* (although the causal circle may be more difficult to establish with the former, and the implausibility of self-exemplification may be more difficult to establish with the latter).

Furthermore, consider God's haecceity, the property *being God*. The property *being necessarily exemplified* is contained in the essence of this property. So, when God causes his haecceity to exist, he causes the property *being necessarily exemplified* to be exemplified by his haecceity. Just as God causes *being red* to be exemplified by the table when he causes it to exist, God causes *being God* to be exemplified necessarily. However, one might well think this incoherent. Indeed, it seems this is the divine causing his own existence: God is pulling himself up by his own bootstraps.

The theistic emanationist needs to address these sorts of concerns about bootstrapping, and it is not clear how that could be done.

8.3.3 Theistic Mentalism without Divine Simplicity

Theistic Mentalism (without Divine Simplicity): Necessarily existing abstracta are identical with divine mental states, and God isn't simple. (Example: Welty 2014.)

One sort of theistic mentalism is the view that necessarily existing abstract objects are divine mental states and that God isn't simple.[5] On this view, God is distinct from his mental states, and abstracta are identical with these mental states. One proponent of this view is Greg Welty (2014). He says,

> I maintain that [abstract objects] are constitutively dependent on God, for they are constituted by the divine ideas, which inhere in the divine mind and have no existence outside it ... [Abstract objects] are necessarily existing, uncreated divine ideas that are distinct from God and dependent on God. (Welty 2014, p. 81)

Why might someone adopt theistic mentalism? One could make the following sort of case. Thoughts (e.g., sentences in the language of thought) are capable of representing the world as being a particular way. Propositions are capable of representing the world as being a particular way. Why do we need both of these sorts of intentional entities? We can simply identify propositions and thoughts, and we get a simpler ontology.

There are *prima facie* concerns with an attempt to identify propositions and thoughts. If the thoughts we speak of here are human thoughts, there are (at least!) continuum-many true propositions and finitely many human thoughts. Furthermore, there are propositions true in worlds where there are no human thoughts. Thus, there are initial obstacles to identifying propositions and human thoughts.

However, we don't have this problem with divine thoughts. God, we may grant, exists necessarily. And God has sufficiently many mental states to stand in for true propositions (see Plantinga 1980, 1982, for discussion).

If we identify propositions with divine thoughts, we have enough of them in all possible situations. And one has fewer kinds of things if one admits only thoughts (divine and otherwise) rather than thoughts and propositions. But there are reasons to think that there are both thoughts and propositions and that the two shouldn't be identified. The most straightforward reason is that thoughts are a different kind of entity from propositions. The former are concrete, and the latter are abstract. Furthermore, it's worth noting the conceptual role propositions play. They are the sorts of things that can be affirmed, doubted, believed, and questioned. They can be true and false, necessary and possible. It is said by some that they are sets of possible worlds; and by others that they are composite entities, made up of properties and relations, and perhaps concrete individuals. It's not at all clear that thoughts, even divine thoughts, satisfy these conceptual roles.

We also should ask about other necessarily existing abstracta. What sorts of mental entities are they? Do they relate to one another, as concrete mental tokens; in the right sort of way such that they mirror the ways that Platonic states of affairs, propositions, properties, relations, and numbers relate to one another?

What these considerations suggest is that theistic mentalism may actually be a sort of nominalism about abstract objects, in the way that Plantinga (1987) says Lewis's (1986) conception of possible worlds is a sort of nominalism about possible worlds. At best, we have concrete things that attempt to play the roles of necessarily existing abstract objects. (And the theistic mentalist has a great deal more work in specifying concrete divine mental particulars such that we have all the requisite role-players among the various sorts of necessarily existing abstract objects. It is presumably not enough to say that propositions are divine thoughts and leave it at that.)

Let us return to the initial motivation for theistic mentalism: There are two sorts of intentional objects (propositions and thoughts), and it would be a simpler metaphysic to identify tokens of the two sorts. To assess this, we must ask if the tokens of the two sorts are enough like each other to be identified. When we consider the virtues of a metaphysic, simplicity isn't the only relevant consideration. After all, Spinoza's metaphysic (necessarily there is one object that is exactly as it is in the actual world) is maximally simple yet has few proponents within Western philosophy. Furthermore, if we are able to explain the intentionality of one of these sorts of entities by its relation to the other, it will seem less mysterious that we have two classes of intentional entities. That is precisely what many want to say about the intentionality of thoughts *vis-à-vis* that of propositions: Thoughts derive their intentionality by standing in the right sort of relation to propositions. So, the reason why my thought is a thought that grass is green is because it has the propositional content *grass is green*. The proposition *grass is green* has its intentionality intrinsically.

8.3.4 Theistic Mentalism with Divine Simplicity

Theistic Mentalism (with Divine Simplicity): Necessarily existing abstracta are identical with divine mental states, and God is simple. (Examples: Augustine, Aquinas, Avicenna.)

Theistic mentalism with divine simplicity is the view that necessarily existing abstracta are identical with divine mental states and that God is simple. Because God is simple, each abstract object is identical with God and thus each other. This is a view held most famously by Augustine and Aquinas.[6]

Because this is a mentalist view, the criticisms leveled in the section on theistic mentalism without divine simplicity will apply here. In addition, the person who accepts divine simplicity alongside her divine mentalism will face criticisms of divine simplicity. Plantinga (1980) is perhaps the locus classicus of contemporary criticism of divine simplicity. He argues that according to divine simplicity, God is identical with his attributes and has (all of) his attributes essentially. But, he argues, God isn't an attribute and God has many different attributes. (For discussions more sympathetic to divine simplicity, see Bergmann and Brower 2006; Leftow 1990b; Mann 1982; Stump 2010; Stump and Kretzmann 1985; Wolterstorff 1991.) The sorts of difficulties that Plantinga has raised have seemed decisive to many. But there are perhaps further objections for the theistic mentalist who embraces divine simplicity, however. It will be difficult for one to deny that God is distinct from God's thoughts without admitting that God isn't simple. If this is so, then the theistic mentalist who embraces divine simplicity is committed to saying that God is identical with each abstract object. Thus, the theistic mentalist who accepts divine simplicity has, *prima facie*, a great number of difficulties with her view.

8.4 Views on Which It's Not the Case That All Necessarily Existing Abstracta Are Grounded in God

8.4.1 Theistic Platonism

Theistic Platonism: There are necessarily existing abstract objects, and none of them are grounded in God. (Example: van Inwagen 2009).

According to the theistic Platonist, there are necessarily existing abstract objects, the existence and nature of which are not grounded in God. Peter van Inwagen (2009) is a paradigm case of a theistic Platonist. As we saw earlier, van Inwagen argues that if necessarily existing abstract objects were grounded in God, they would be caused to exist by God. But necessarily existing abstracta can't enter into causal relations. So they aren't grounded in God. He says,

> In the end, I can find no sense in the idea that God creates free abstract objects [things like propositions, relations, numbers, properties, etc.], no sense in the idea that the existence of free abstract objects in some way depends on the activities of God. (Recall that, although I believe that all abstract objects are free, that is not a position that I am concerned to defend in this chapter.) And that is because the existence of free abstract objects depends on nothing. Their existence has nothing to do with causation ... Causation is simply irrelevant to the being (and the intrinsic properties) of abstract objects. (van Inwagen 2009, p. 18)

Van Inwagen takes his most serious challenge to be from religious texts that he, as a Christian, thinks are authoritative. He speaks particularly of the beginning of the Niceno-Constantinopolitan Creed, which begins, "I believe in one God, the Father almighty, maker of heaven and earth, of all that is seen and unseen." He thinks here that the quantifier in "all that is seen and unseen" is restricted to things that are capable of entering into causal relations and thus are capable of being created. As van Inwagen points out, there are other authoritative Christian texts in which a universal quantifier is read in a restricted manner (e.g., Matthew 19:26: "for with God all things are possible"; see also Luke 1:37, Mark 10:27). No such passage should be taken as a proof text for a Cartesian view of omnipotence. Rather, the quantifier is read in a restricted manner. Similarly, the quantifier is restricted in the case of the beginning of the Niceno-Constantinopolitan Creed.

It is worth noting that van Inwagen's argument here is slightly different from one that often occurs around these sorts of texts. Often, there is discussion as to whether the writers of the authoritative texts had in mind things like necessarily existing abstracta (e.g., Morris and Menzel 1986, p. 354; Wolterstorff 1970, p. 293). To the person who says that the writers of these texts didn't have, say, structured propositions in mind when they claimed God created everything, it is pointed out that neither did they have in mind (clearly created) things like quarks and bosons (e.g., Davidson 1999, pp. 278–9). Rather, van Inwagen argues that a text like the beginning of the Niceno-Constantinopolitan Creed has to be read in a restricted manner if it is to avoid asserting impossible propositions. And this seems the right way to go for the theistic Platonist. It is very difficult to discern the scope of the universal quantifier in the usage of writers from nearly 2,000 years ago. (This is apart from questions about the connection between intention and semantic content.)

Van Inwagen's main focus is on authoritative texts like the Niceno-Constantinopolitan Creed. But we noted earlier a second sort of reason for adopting a view on which any necessarily existing abstract objects depend on God. That second sort of reason is perfect-being theology. Again, the line of reasoning is that a being who is such that necessarily existing abstracta depend on it is greater than a being on whom they don't depend. And God is the greatest possible being. It is clear what van Inwagen would say at this point: It's not possible for necessarily existing abstract objects to depend on anything.

Thus, *being an x such that necessarily existing abstracta depend on x* is not a great-making property. That this isn't a great-making property is the sort of thing the theistic Platonist needs to say to the perfect-being defender of divine grounding of necessarily existing abstracta. It must be that these things can't depend on God or anyone else. (One may or may not adopt van Inwagen's particular argument that they can't.)

Thus, if the theistic Platonist thinks there are good arguments that necessarily existing abstract objects can't be grounded in God, she will have reason to do two things. First, she will have reason to read the relevant universal quantifications in authoritative texts as restricted. Second, if she accepts the sort of reasoning in perfect being theology, she will have reason to insist that *being an x such that necessarily existing abstracta depend on x* is not a great-making property (any more than *being able to create a square circle* is).

8.4.2 Theistic Nominalism

Theistic Nominalism: There are no necessarily existing abstract objects. (Example: Craig 2016.)

The theistic nominalist doesn't think there are necessarily existing abstract objects. She may or may not think if there were necessarily existing abstract objects, they would be grounded in God. For instance, William Lane Craig (2016) who is a theistic nominalist; thinks that were there necessarily existing abstracta, they would have to be grounded in God. (We presumably should count Craig as someone who thinks there are true counterpossibles.) But one can imagine someone who thinks that if things like numbers and properties did exist, theistic Platonism would be a plausible view to adopt. It is worth noting that very few—if any—of the realists about necessarily existing abstracta who are theists are themselves realists *because* they are theists. Rather, they are realists about necessarily existing abstracta for other sorts of reasons (e.g., indispensability arguments, arguments that we quantify over them with true sentences, or arguments that true sentences [e.g., that 2 + 3 = 5] require them as truthmakers). Van Inwagen himself believes in necessarily existing abstract objects because he thinks that we are committed to ineliminable existential quantifications over them (e.g., van Inwagen 2014b, ch. 8). There is nothing in particular the theistic nominalist needs to say *qua* theist about the existence of necessarily existing abstracta that any other nominalist doesn't need to say. One advantage of theistic nominalism is that it allows one to avoid some of the sorts of difficult maneuvers that those who believe God grounds the existence of necessarily existing abstract objects wind up performing. Another advantage of theistic nominalism is that it allows one, if she wishes, to avoid some debates about the semantics of universal quantifiers in ancient religious texts. Of course, theistic nominalism is open only to those who find plausible nominalistic replies to standard arguments for realism about necessarily existing abstracta. Craig himself thinks that he can give replies to these standard arguments for realism (Craig 2016, chs. 3, 6, 7).

We turn now to two "Mixed Views," views on which different types of abstracta stand in different grounding relations to God. Both of them try to bracket abstracta having to do with God (e.g., God's own attributes) and to say that God doesn't ground those. But God grounds all the other necessarily existing abstracta.

8.4.3 Mixed View 1: Mentalism-Platonism

Mixed View 1: Mentalism-Platonism: Mentalism is true of propositions. Other abstracta are independent of God. (Example: Gould and Davis 2014.) On this view, propositions are identical with divine mental states, and properties and relations not exemplified by God are independent of God, *à la* theistic Platonism. This is the view of Gould and Davis (2014). They say, "Thus, abstract objects exist in two realms: the divine mind and Plato's heaven" (Gould and Davis 2014, p. 61). They decline to say in this particular essay whether mentalism or Platonism is true of other sorts of abstract objects (e.g., numbers, states of affairs, possible worlds). So what we have in Gould and Davis is an initial sketch of a proposal. They are motivated by bootstrapping worries for theistic activism (itself an emanationist view). They think that they can evade bootstrapping objections by having some abstracta be identical with divine mental states and having the others not grounded in God. Their own name for this view is "modified theistic activism."

It is perhaps strange that, having started with theistic activism (an emanationist view) and its bootstrapping worries, they wind up with a part-mentalist view. It would seem that they could have kept some abstracta causally grounded in God and others independent of God (see Mixed View 2 next). Also, this first Mixed View will face objections of the sort faced by theistic Platonism; namely, that it doesn't take divine aseity seriously enough and that it must read the quantifiers in the relevant religious texts in a restricted manner. Furthermore, it is peculiar that propositions wind up as divine mental states, but properties and relations wind up independent of God. One natural understanding of propositions (that we have adopted in this book) is that they are structured entities, made up of properties and relations. Another is that they are sets of possible worlds. The former understanding seems unavailable to Gould and Davis, and the latter would seem to involve having *sui generis* primitive possible worlds identical with divine mental states. But at that point, why not just be a thoroughgoing theistic mentalist? After all, bootstrapping isn't a concern for the mentalist. Furthermore, bootstrapping worries arise with abstracta other than properties. For instance, consider the proposition *God is omnipotent*. In any possible world it exists, it is true. That is, it has *being true* as part of its essence. But then, if God causes it to exist, God causes it to be true. So we have the same sorts of bootstrapping concerns as we did with a property like *being omnipotent*.

8.4.4 Mixed View 2: Anti-Bootstrapping Emanationism

Mixed View 2: Anti-Bootstrapping Emanationism: Any abstracta that create "bootstrapping" problems aren't grounded in God. Theistic emanationism is true of the others.

This is a view designed wholly to avoid bootstrapping worries that affect theistic emanationism. It *really* is a sort of modified theistic activism, and it may actually be the sort of view Gould and Davis would like to hold. The idea is this: Ascertain the necessarily existing abstracta that cause bootstrapping problems (e.g., *being God, being omnipotent*) for the emanationist. Those exist independently of God. All other necessarily existing abstracta are causally grounded in God in the way the theistic emanationist thinks abstracta are grounded in God.

So far as I can tell, no one holds this second Mixed View. This might have to do with the fact that it seems quite *ad hoc*: The sole motivation for the two classes of abstracta in the theory is avoidance of bootstrapping worries.

But this accusation of ad-hocness is perhaps too swift. There is a reason why certain abstracta create bootstrapping problems. That reason is that they have to do with God in a way that other abstracta that don't cause bootstrapping problems don't. So why not say that Leibniz or Morris and Menzel are right about all the non-God-related abstracta? To put it another way, why not be an emanationist about all the abstracta one can be an emanationist about—those that don't have to do with God?

That said, there is at least a whiff of ad-hocness here. The motivation for this theory presumably would be that of perfect being theology. The proponent of this Mixed View must think that the quantifiers in relevant religious texts are actually restricted. They aren't as restricted as the theistic Platonist thinks they are. But she will agree with the theistic Platonist that it's false that all (read the quantifier wide open) entities are created by/depend on/grounded in God. It's worth pointing out that it's not clear how to delineate precisely those abstracta that lead to bootstrapping problems and those that don't. The best one can do seems to be to say that those that cause bootstrapping problems don't depend on God, and all others God causes to exist. But presumably for each necessarily existing abstract object, either it gives rise to bootstrapping problems or it doesn't. So there should be two nonoverlapping classes of abstract objects at hand here, even if we're not able to specify more descriptively which abstracta are in which class.

It would be better if the emanationist could find a cogent reply to bootstrapping concerns. But if she can't, she may plump for being an emanationist about all abstracta save those having to do with God.

8.5 Analysis

Which of these views should the theist adopt? I personally have never felt the pull of the motivations that it is important that God be responsible for the existence and nature of necessarily existing abstract objects. It's not that I don't sympathize with some cases where it is claimed that God ought to be responsible for a putative necessary existent. Newton thought that space was an infinite necessary existent. I understand the motivation for saying this sort of necessary existent depends on God. Newton himself identified space with

God's omnipresence, which led some to accuse him of holding a view very close to pantheism. But I can see why one would want to say that God grounds the existence of space, whatever space's metaphysical status. However, with propositions, numbers, states of affairs, and the rest of the Platonic horde, I don't think it sacrifices God's aseity that these things are not grounded in God. They are the backdrop against and with which God exercises his creative activity in bringing into existence contingent beings. It also seems to me that there are serious problems, detailed earlier, with theistic voluntarism and theistic emanationism. Thus, were I tempted by a view in which God grounds the existence of necessarily existing abstracta, it'd be theistic mentalism. But I'm not so tempted and thus think that the theist ought to be a theistic Platonist. I don't, however, agree with van Inwagen that the acausality of abstracta rules them out as objects of divine production. Indeed, abstract objects enter into causal relations all the time. Thus, I don't have some of the objections to theistic voluntarism and theistic emanationism that van Inwagen has. But the view he defends strikes me as the most plausible on the menu.[7]

Notes

Introduction

1 See Roy and Davidson (2012) for some of my thoughts on the nature of progress in philosophy.

1 Independence Actualism Explicated

1 Thus, Meinongianism is equivalent to *possibilism* in Plantinga's (2003b, p. 179) and others' use of that term. I don't mean to imply that Meinongianism is precisely what Meinong himself believed, though he was a Meinongian in our sense of the term.
2 Though the first use of the word "actualism," according to Adams, is found in Williams (1959).
3 Peter van Inwagen (2012) reports Robert Adams as telling him that he regrets his 1981 definition of actualism and prefers something closer to his 1974 definition.
4 Though Menzel (2020) argues that they are possibilists and that our definition of actualism should reflect this.
5 See also Lambert (2003, ch. 8).

2 The Independence Thesis

1 Defenders of serious actualism (the term originates with Plantinga 1979) include Plantinga (1979, 1983, 1985a, 1985b); Merricks (2015); Adams (1981); Stalnaker (2012); Menzel (1991); Deutsch (1994); Prior (1957); Prior and Fine (1977); Davidson (2000); and Bergmann (1996, 1999). Opponents of it include Salmon (1987, 1998); Pollock (1984, 1985); Fine (1985), Hinchliff (1988); Soames (2002); and Fitch (1988).
2 Defenders of serious presentism include Prior (1957), Bergmann (1999), Davidson (2003b), and Crisp (2005). Opponents include Hinchliff (1988). Formulations of serious actualism and presentism usually are equivalent to that which we just saw. But with each there is an (often unstated explicitly) additional

component: That actualism or presentism is true. Thus, we will take serious actualism to entail actualism and serious presentism to entail presentism.
3 This would be so either because independence actualism would be necessarily false or would be too weak to do the work we want it to do. Suppose that presentism and actualism are both necessarily true, as are serious presentism and serious actualism. Then the independence thesis would be necessarily false. Suppose, though, eternalism is true in some worlds and presentism is true in others. (That these theories of time aren't true of necessity is a substantial metaphysical claim, but grant it for the example.) Call a world where eternalism is true, W_E. As before, assume that serious actualism is necessarily true; thus it is true in W_E. It also might be true that in any world W_P where presentism is true, no objects have properties at times at which they don't exist. Thus, in W_P, serious presentism and serious actualism would both be true. Nevertheless, it might be true in W_E that entities have properties at times where they don't exist—that is, at times where none of their temporal parts are located. Thus, one could conceive a model where serious presentism and serious actualism both were true (each holds at every world where presentism and actualism hold, respectively) and the independence thesis also was true. But, as we shall see in Chapter 3, the applications for which one employs the independence thesis involve a more robust distribution of properties to objects than we have in this model. Thus, serious actualism and serious presentism, if true, would spell real problems at least for the utility of (if not the possible truth of) independence actualism.
4 The argument I give here is a statement from Plantinga (1983) of the original Plantinga (1979) argument. This is to keep numbering of premises consistent in this chapter and to make the inference between (14) and (15) clear.
5 Bergmann equates being in w with having being in w.
6 I'm reminded of something I once heard Richard Foley say in a talk: "That's not a counterexample. That's my view."
7 Stephanou's own statement of the arguments make heavy use of quantified modal logic symbolism. I think that I can state it adequately mostly in English and will render it that way.
8 Stephanou relies on some reasoning earlier on the paper to show this premise. I'm going to assume that it's unobjectionable, though I encourage the reader to look at Stephanou's reasoning for more detail.
9 Yagisawa uses "Fx" rather than "x having F," but the change won't matter for our purposes here.
10 It's true that Lewis has his recombination principle that is supposed to get him at least some of the concrete worlds he thinks he needs. But the principle is made-to-order to do just that and doesn't serve as any sort of independent reason for thinking the concrete worlds have the features he needs them to have.

3 The Utility of Independence Actualism

1. Note that a problem remains for the presentist even if singular propositions like (P1) have necessarily existing individual essences (like haecceities) as constituents rather than concrete objects like events. Even if one has a complete proposition that we are evaluating, there still is the question of how the proposition in question can be true.
2. Mark Hinchliff addresses problems for presentism with a *prima facie* similar strategy. But as we saw in Chapter 1, he's a Meinongian. The independence actualist and Hinchliff agree that non-present objects have properties and stand in relations. But he thinks he quantifies over non-present objects with his widest quantifiers. The independence actualist denies that there are nonexistent objects.
3. The independence actualist may plump for a similar reply to problems for presentism from special relativity.
4. The Sib case is a variant of Nathan Salmon's (1987) Noman case, though I use a blastocyst rather than the sperm and egg pre-fertilization that Salmon uses. I think this makes it harder to deny that we can entertain the requisite singular propositions. The conversation with God is designed to make it even harder to do so. I'm assuming two things here. First, I'm assuming living persons are never identical with early-stage blastocysts. Second, I'm assuming Kripkean-type intuitions about the impossibility of distinct people coming from the same blastocyst (at the very least in nearby worlds).
5. Mark is my real brother.
6. Braun himself picked up the idea from David Kaplan's "Demonstratives" (Kaplan 2007b).
7. In Braun (1993) he has sets as parts of propositions; the notation here is that of his work in 2005. The views are equivalent for our purposes.
8. The specter of this hybrid sort propositional picture seems to have been a major reason why Russell abandoned his 1903 metaphysics (see Grossman 1974 and Griffin 1986 for discussion).
9. This is the view of Plantinga (1974). See Davidson (2003a) for discussion.
10. I'm sidestepping issues about existentialism here.
11. See Freddoso 1988, Flint 1998, and throughout Persyzk 2011 for further discussion of this problem for Molinism.

4 Actualism or Meinongianism?

1. And showing the preferability of independence actualism over Meinongianism is the goal of this chapter.

2. This isn't to say that Russell in the *Principles* held to Meinong's entire metaphysics. It is rather to say that he was a Meinongian in our sense of the term (i.e., he thought there were nonexistent objects).
3. I discuss these in Chapter 3.
4. Again, see Section 3.3 for more discussion of negative existentials.
5. Or at least the right sort of Meinongian does. See Chapter 7 for further discussion.
6. I personally think that some truth-in-fiction analysis of fictional discourse is preferable. But what is important for my purposes in this chapter is to show that the independence actualist is not worse off with respect to fictional discourse than is the Meinongian.

5 "Exists" as a Predicate

1. In the rest of the chapter, I will omit references to cognates of "exists" and will speak just of "exists."
2. There of course is the question of how "exists" behaves in sentences like "cars exist." It may seem obvious that "exists" is second order in this sort of case. But we could take "cars" to be a plural referring term and the sentence to involve a first-order predication about those things. I am concerned with singular sentences in this chapter because they most easily give rise to worries about nonexistent objects and singular predication. In this I follow nearly the entirety of the debate back to the eighteenth century.
3. I don't mean to exclude nominalists from holding the second-order view. But I find the second-order view easiest to characterize, especially given the way it is generally characterized in the literature, with Platonist language. All I say here can be translated into metalinguistic talk that avoids Platonistic ontological commitments. But that gets cumbersome, so I will talk as though there are propositions, individual essences, and the like.
4. So, View 1 is the first-order view, and View 2 is the second-order view.
5. I do not assume that those I go on to discuss would necessarily agree with my characterization (in terms of structured propositions) of the difference between existence being a first- or second-order predicate. But, as we will see, the basic concepts all employ are the same: predication of existence directly of an object versus instantiation or exemplification of a property or something like a property (an individual essence or concept).
6. It's worth noting that the defender of a second-order view would (or could) say that while the content of "Horses" is a property of some sort, the statement is about the class of things that exemplify the property, namely, horses.

7 I do not here mean to take a position on the success of the attempted naming.
8 We will discuss them further in Chapter 8.
9 See Dixon (2018) for discussion of this.
10 Thanks to James Van Cleve for the reference.
11 Reinhardt Grossmann (1984, p. 397) gives an argument of a similar flavor.
12 Presumably, we don't "get them to exist," as McGinn says, but rather they already exist independently of us.
13 See Soames (2002) for discussion of Kripke's arguments.
14 Frege seems to have thought that the idea of there being propositions with concrete individuals as constituents made no sense. See his dialogue with Russell (in Davidson 2007a, p. 53). But surely, if Frege even is right about the semantics of natural languages, it's a contingent fact that he is. We could have had concrete objects as semantic values for rigid terms. Then, presumably the meanings of sentences that contain those rigid terms would have concrete objects as part of them. Thus, the insistence on the incoherence of singular propositions is a really strong claim that tells against either structured propositions or the contingency of our semantic practices.

6 Existence and Essence

1 Plantinga distinguishes between quidditative properties and propositions, "which make direct reference" to an individual, and qualitative properties and propositions, which don't. (We will eschew issues of reference occurring outside of linguistic items or speech acts.) I discuss the nature of quidditative properties in Davidson (forthcoming).
2 Direct aboutness of a similar sort (though he doesn't think there are Russellian singular propositions) is at the core of what a singular proposition is, according to Trenton Merricks (2015).
3 I explore and defend a view on which haecceities have as constituents objects that exemplify them in Davidson (forthcoming).
4 Rosenkrantz (1993) makes a similar argument.
5 Sometimes in the literature, "Hume's Dictum" is used for another principle: There is no necessary connection between (exemplifications of) distinct properties. Sometimes it is used for the conjunction of this second principle and what I'm calling "Hume's Dictum." So there isn't uniformity on the semantics of the term. But most of the time (I think) it is used as I use it. See Van Cleve (forthcoming) for a comprehensive discussion of Hume's Dictum (and other similar principles) and its use in contemporary philosophy.

6 Presumably, there is no problem with Hume's Dictum if the haecceity exists necessarily.
7 Van Cleve (forthcoming) modifies Hume's Dictum in this way.
8 This sort of argument is discussed in many places, for example, Prior (1976), Adams (1981), Fine (1985), Pollock (1984, 1985), Plantinga (1979, 1983, 1985a), Fitch (1988), Davidson (2000), Williamson (2002), King (2007), Stalnaker (2010, 2012), Speaks (2012), and Merricks (2015).
9 I've modified slightly Plantinga's original argument for ease of exposition.
10 I give a version of this sort of argument for the possibility of unexemplified haecceities in Davidson (forthcoming, ch. 5).
11 I want to use something closer to Fine's language to mark this concept just because in ordinary possible worlds discourse "in" and "at" are often used interchangeably.
12 Sib (from Chapter 3) is an individual who would come to be from a particular blastocyst.
13 Again, throughout this discussion of Plantinga's argument against existentialism, it is assumed that serious actualism is true.
14 Thanks to Tom Crisp for the objection.
15 Fine's own reply is complicated and beyond the scope of this chapter. I refer the reader to it in Fine (2005, pp. 335 ff.).

7 Robust and Deflationary Meinongianism

1 We should note that Thomas Reid seems to be a Robust Meinongian before Meinong was.
2 Meinong himself in his later work seems to have looked favorably on this sort of solution. See Jacquette (2015, ch. 5) for discussion.
3 Rather than speak of properties, I could speak of sets of objects that satisfy a predicate (so as to please the nominalist). But I find it less cumbersome to speak as though there are properties that are the semantic contents of predicates, and so will do so.
4 It's worth pointing out that giving an analysis of a fundamental relation like exemplification is a tall order for anyone.
5 Everett (2013) raises related problems for Zalta's theory from its positing of ambiguity in natural language.
6 Following Routley, Priest calls his theory "noneism." His theory is quite different from Routley's though, in that nonexistent objects exemplify very few properties.

Berto (2012) defends a view very much like Priest's. What I have to say here about Priest's view will apply to Berto's view *mutatis mutandis*.

7 One might imagine Meinong granting that there is an existing golden mountain but insisting that we shouldn't expect to notice it. Perhaps it's just really far away, for example, on the other side of the galaxy. The problem with this reply is that we can just modify the definite description in question to have the golden mountain nearby. Then we really would expect to find it.

8 The argument here is employed against views on which fictional characters are abstracta, though immediately after this paragraph, Everett raises the same concerns for Meinongianism.

9 Similarly, perhaps it's a necessary truth that the nonexistent planet Vulcan orbits a nonexistent sun.

8 God and Necessary Existence

1 All references to the Hebrew Bible and New Testament are from the New Revised Standard Version of the Bible.

2 See Friedell (2020) for good reasons for thinking van Inwagen is wrong about abstracta having causal powers.

3 For instance, they might think that if A depends on B, then if B didn't exist, A wouldn't exist, and not conversely. But according to the Lewis's semantics for counterfactuals, if A and B exist necessarily, then if A didn't exist, neither would B, and conversely. See Wierenga (1998), Vander Laan (2004), Mares (1997), and Nolan (1997) for alternative semantics for counterfactuals with necessarily false antecedents ("counterpossibles").

4 There are those who demur, though. See, for example, Chandler (1976) and Salmon (1981, App. 1).

5 This view is sometimes called "divine conceptualism," but often on this view, divine mental states other than concepts are pointed to as being identical with abstracta. For this reason, we will use the term "mentalism" rather than "conceptualism."

6 For Augustine's mentalism, see "On Ideas," Q 46. For Augustine on divine simplicity, see *City of God* XI, 10. For Aquinas's mentalism, see "Disputed Questions on Truth," Q3 Art 1, and *Summa Theologica* 1 Q15. For Aquinas on divine simplicity, see *Summa Theologica* 1.3 and "Disputed Questions," I.7.6.

7 The content in this chapter overlaps that of Davidson (2019).

Bibliography

Adams, Fred, and Robert Stecker. "Vacuous Singular Terms." *Mind and Language* 9, no. 4 (1994): 387–401.
Adams, Fred, Gary Fuller, and Robert Stecker. "The Semantics of Fictional Names." *Pacific Philosophical Quarterly* 78, no. 2 (1997): 128–48.
Adams, Robert M. "Theories of Actuality." *Noûs* 8, no. 3 (1974): 211–31.
Adams, Robert M. "Middle Knowledge and the Problem of Evil." *American Philosophical Quarterly* 14, no. 2 (1977): 109–17.
Adams, Robert M. "Primitive Thisness and Primitive Identity." *Journal of Philosophy* 76, no. 1 (1979): 5–26.
Adams, Robert M. "Actualism and Thisness." *Synthese* 49, no. 1 (1981): 3–41.
Aquinas, Thomas. *Summa Theologica*. Translated by Fathers of the Dominican Province. Westminster: Christian Classics, 1948.
Aquinas, Thomas. *Disputed Questions on Truth*. Translated by R. W. Mulligan. Chicago: Regnery, 1952.
Audi, Paul. "A Clarification and Defense of the Notion of Grounding." In *Metaphysical Grounding: Understanding the Structure of Reality*, edited by Fabrice Correia and Benjamin Schnieder, 101–21. Cambridge: Cambridge University Press, 2012.
Augustine. *The City of God*. Translated by Marcus Dods. New York: Barnes and Noble, 2006.
Ayer, A. J. *Language, Truth and Logic*. New York: Dover, 1952.
Ayer, A. J. *Logical Positivism*. Glencoe: Free Press, 1959.
Bencivenga, Ermanno. "Free Logics." In *Handbook of Philosophical Logic*, edited by D. M. Gabbay and F. Guenthner, 2nd ed., vol. 3, 373–427. Dordrecht: Kluwer Academic Publishers, 2002.
Bennett, Karen. "Proxy 'Actualism.'" *Philosophical Studies* 129, no. 2 (2006): 263–94.
Bergmann, Michael. "A New Argument from Actualism to Serious Actualism." *Noûs* 30, no. 3 (1996): 356–9.
Bergmann, Michael. "(Serious) Actualism and (Serious) Presentism." *Noûs* 33, no. 1 (1999): 118–32.
Bergmann, Michael, and Jeffrey E. Brower. "A Theistic Argument against Platonism (and in Support of Truthmakers and Divine Simplicity)." *Oxford Studies in Metaphysics* 2 (2006): 357–86.

Berkeley, George. *Berkeley's Commonplace Book*. London: Faber & Faber Limited, 1930.

Berto, Francesco. *Existence as a Real Property*. Dordrecht: Springer, 2012.

Berto, Francesco, and Graham Priest. "Modal Meinongianism and Characterization." *Grazer Philosophische Studien* 90 (2014): 183–200.

Berto, Francesco, Filippo Casati, Naoya Fujikawa, Graham Priest. "Modal Meinongianism and Object Theory." *Australasian Journal of Logic* 17 (2020): 1–21.

Bigelow, John. "Presentism and Properties." *Philosophical Perspectives* 10 (1996): 35–52.

Braun, David. "Empty Names." *Noûs* 27, no. 4 (1993): 449–69.

Braun, David. "Empty Names, Fictional Names, Mythical Names." *Noûs* 39, no. 4 (2005): 596–631.

Bricker, Phillip. "Absolute Actuality and the Plurality of Worlds." *Philosophical Perspectives* 20 (2006): 41–76.

Bueno, Otavio, and Edward Zalta. "Object Theory and Modal Meinongianism." *Australasian Journal of Philosophy* 95, no. 4 (2017): 761–78.

Cameron, Ross P. *The Moving Spotlight: An Essay on Time and Ontology*. Oxford: Oxford University Press, 2015.

Caplan, Ben. "Millian Descriptivism." *Philosophical Studies* 133, no. 2 (2007): 181–98.

Caplan, Ben, and David Sanson. "The Way Things Were." *Philosophy and Phenomenological Research* 81, no. 1 (2010): 24–39.

Carnap, Rudolph. "The Elimination of Metaphysics through Logical Analysis of Language." In *Logical Positivism*, edited by A. J. Ayer, 60–82. Glencoe: Free Press, 1959.

Cartwright, Richard L. "Negative Existentials." *Journal of Philosophy* 57, nos. 20/21 (1960): 629–39.

Chandler, Hugh S. "Plantinga and the Contingently Possible." *Analysis* 36, no. 2 (1976): 106–9.

Chisholm, Roderick M., ed. *Realism and the Background of Phenomenology*. Glencoe: Free Press, 1960.

Chisholm, Roderick M. "Homeless Objects." *Revue Internationale de Philosophie* 27, nos. 104/105 (1973): 207–23.

Chisholm, Roderick. "Self-Profile." In *Roderick M. Chisholm*, edited by R. Bogdan, 3–81. Dordrecht: Reidel, 1986.

Church, Alonzo. *Introduction to Mathematical Logic*. Princeton: Princeton University Press, 1956.

Cocchiarella, Nino. "Quantification, Time, and Necessity." In *Philosophical Applications of Free Logic*, edited by Karel Lambert, 242–57. Oxford: Oxford University Press, 1991.

Craig, William L. *God over All: Divine Aseity and the Challenge of Platonism*. Oxford: Oxford University Press, 2016.

Crane, Tim. *The Objects of Thought*. Oxford: Oxford University Press, 2013.

Crisp, Thomas M. "Presentism and "Cross-Time" Relations." *American Philosophical Quarterly* 42, no. 1 (2005): 5–17.

Crisp, Thomas M. "Presentism and the Grounding Objection." *Noûs* 41, no. 1 (2007): 90–109.

Cruse, D. A. *Lexical Semantics*. Cambridge: Cambridge University Press, 1997.

Daly, Chris. "Scepticism about Grounding." In *Metaphysical Grounding: Understanding the Structure of Reality*, edited by Fabrice Correia and Benjamin Schnieder, 81–101. Cambridge: Cambridge University Press, 2012.

Davidson, Matthew. "A Demonstration against Theistic Activism." *Religious Studies* 35, no. 3 (1999): 277–90.

Davidson, Matthew. "Direct Reference and Singular Propositions." *American Philosophical Quarterly* 37, no. 3 (2000): 285–300.

Davidson, Matthew. "Introduction." In *Essays in the Metaphysics of Modality* by Alvin Plantinga, edited by Matthew Davidson, 1–25. New York: Oxford University Press, 2003a.

Davidson, Matthew. "Presentism and the Non-present." *Philosophical Studies* 113, no. 1 (2003b): 77–92.

Davidson, Matthew, ed. *On Sense and Direct Reference*. New York: McGraw Hill, 2007a.

Davidson, Matthew. "Transworld Identity, Singular Propositions, and Picture Thinking." In *On Sense and Direct Reference*, edited by Matthew Davidson, 559–69. New York: McGraw Hill, 2007b.

Davidson, Matthew. "Presentism and Grounding Past Truths." In *New Papers on the Present: Focus on Presentism*, edited by Roberto Ciuni, Giuliano Torrengo, and Kristie Miller, 153–72. Munich: Verlag, 2013.

Davidson, Matthew. "God and Other Necessary Beings." In *Stanford Encyclopedia of Philosophy*, edited by Edward Zalta. Summer 2019. https://plato.stanford.edu/entries/god-necessary-being/.

Davidson, Matthew. *About Haecceity: An Essay in Ontology*. Forthcoming.

Davison, Scott A. "Could Abstract Objects Depend upon God?" *Religious Studies* 27, no. 4 (1991): 485–97.

De Molina, Luis. *On Divine Foreknowledge: Part IV of the Concordia*. Edited by Alfred J. Freddoso. Ithaca: Cornell University Press, 1988.

Descartes, René. *The Philosophical Works of Descartes*. Edited by Elizabeth S. Haldane and G. R. T. Ross. New York: Dover, 1955.

Descartes, René. *The Philosophical Writings of Descartes*. Translated by John Cottingham, Robert Stoothoff, and Dugald Murdoch. Cambridge: Cambridge University Press, 1991.

Deutsch, Harry. "Logic for Contingent Beings." *Journal of Philosophical Research* 19 (1994): 273–329.

Dixon, T. Scott. "Upward Grounding." *Philosophy and Phenomenological Research* 97, no. 1 (2018): 48–78.

Donnellan, Keith S. "Speaking of Nothing." *Philosophical Review* 83, no. 1 (1974): 249–58.

Everett, Anthony. *The Nonexistent*. Oxford: Oxford University Press, 2013.

Findlay, J. N. *Meinong's Theory of Objects and Values*. Oxford: Oxford University Press, 1963.

Fine, Kit. "Plantinga on the Reduction of Possibilist Discourse." In *Alvin Plantinga*, edited by James Tomberlin and Peter van Inwagen, 145–86. Dordrecht: Springer, 1985.

Fine, Kit. "The Question of Realism." *Philosopher's Imprint* 1 (2001): 1–30.

Fine, Kit. "Necessity and Non-existence." In *Modality and Tense: Philosophical Papers*, 321–57. Oxford: Oxford University Press, 2005.

Fitch, G. W. "The Nature of Singular Propositions." In *Philosophical Analysis: A Defense by Example*, edited by D. F. Austin, 281–99. Dordrecht: Kluwer Academic Publishers, 1988.

Fitch, G. W. "In Defense of Aristotelian Actualism." *Philosophical Perspectives* 10 (1996): 53–71.

Flint, Thomas P. *Divine Providence: The Molinist Account*. Ithaca: Cornell University Press, 1998.

Forrest, Peter. "The Real but Dead Past: A Reply to Braddon-Mitchell." *Analysis* 64, no. 4 (2004): 358–62.

Freddoso, Alfred J. "Introduction." In *On Divine Foreknowledge: Part IV of the Concordia* by Luis De Molina, translated by Alfred J. Freddoso, 1–85. Ithaca: Cornell University Press, 1988.

Frege, Gottlob. *Foundations of Arithmetic*. Evanston: Northwestern University Press, 1986.

Friedell, David. "Abstracta Are Causal." *Philosophia* 48, no. 1 (2020): 133–42.

Gould, Paul M. "Introduction." In *Beyond the Control of God? Six Views on the Problem of God and Abstract Objects*, edited by Paul M. Gould, 1–21. New York: Bloomsbury, 2014.

Gould, Paul M., and Richard B. Davis. "Modified Theistic Activism." In *Beyond the Control of God? Six Views on the Problem of God and Abstract Objects*, edited by Paul M. Gould, 51–64. New York: Bloomsbury, 2014.

Griffin, Nicholas. "Russell's Critique of Meinong's Theory of Objects." *Grazer Philosophische Studien* 25, no. 1 (1986): 375–401.

Grossmann, Reinhardt. "Meinong's Doctrine of the Aussersein of the Pure Object." *Noûs* 8, no. 1 (1974): 67–82.

Grossmann, Reinhardt. *The Categorial Structure of the World*. Bloomington: Indiana University Press, 1984.

Hasker, William. *God, Time and Knowledge*. Ithaca: Cornell University Press, 1989.

Hasker, William. *Providence, Evil and the Openness of God*. London: Routledge, 2004.

Hinchliff, Mark. "A Defense of Presentism." Diss., Princeton University, 1988.

Hofweber, Thomas, and Anthony Everett, eds. *Empty Names, Fiction and the Puzzles of Non-Existence*. Stanford: CSLI Publications, 2000.

Hofweber, Thomas. "Ambitious, yet Modest, Metaphysics." In *Modality: Metaphysics, Logic, and Epistemology*, edited by David J. Chalmers, David Manley, and Ryan Wasserman, 260–89. Oxford: Oxford University Press, 2009.

Hudson, Hud. "On a New Argument from Actualism to Serious Actualism." *Noûs* 31, no. 4 (1997): 520–4.

Hume, David. *A Treatise of Human Nature*. Oxford: Oxford University Press, 1981.

Jacquette, Dale. *Meinongian Logic: The Semantics of Existence and Nonexistence*. Berlin: W. De Gruyter, 1996.

Jacquette, Dale. *Alexius Meinong: The Shepherd of Non-being*. Dordrecht: Springer, 2015.

Jager, Thomas. "An Actualistic Semantics for Quantified Modal Logic." *Notre Dame Journal of Formal Logic* 23, no. 3 (1982): 335–49.

Kant, Immanuel. *The Critique of Pure Reason*. Translated by Norman K. Smith. New York: St. Martin's, 1965.

Kaplan, David. "Afterthoughts." In *On Sense and Direct Reference*, edited by Matthew Davidson, 782–820. New York: McGraw Hill, 2007a.

Kaplan, David. "Demonstratives." In *On Sense and Direct Reference*, edited by Matthew Davidson, 720–82. New York: McGraw Hill, 2007b.

King, Jeffrey C. *The Nature and Structure of Content*. Oxford: Oxford University Press, 2007.

Koslicki, Kathrin. "Varieties of Ontological Dependence." In *Metaphysical Grounding: Understanding the Structure of Reality*, edited by Fabrice Correia and Benjamin Schnieder, 186–213. Cambridge: Cambridge University Press, 2012.

Kripke, Saul. *Naming and Necessity*. Cambridge: Harvard University Press, 1980.

Kripke, Saul. *Reference and Existence*. Oxford: Oxford University Press, 2013.

Kroon, Frederick. "Much Ado about Nothing: Priest and the Reinvention of Noneism." *Philosophy and Phenomenological Research* 76, no. 1 (2008): 199–207.

Lambert, Karel. *Meinong and the Principle of Independence: Its Place in Meinong's Theory of Objects and Its Significance in Contemporary Philosophical Logic*. Cambridge: Cambridge University Press, 1983.

Lambert, Karel. *Free Logic: Selected Essays*. Cambridge: Cambridge University Press, 2003.

Leftow, Brian. "God and Abstract Entities." *Faith and Philosophy* 7, no. 2 (1990a): 193–217.

Leftow, Brian. "Is God an Abstract Object?" *Noûs* 24, no. 4 (1990b): 581–98.

Leibniz, Gottfried. *Philosophical Essays*. Edited by Roger Ariew and Daniel Garber. Indianapolis: Hackett, 1989.

Lewis, David. "Anselm and Actuality." *Noûs* 4, no. 2 (1970): 175–88.

Lewis, David K. *Counterfactuals*. Oxford: Blackwell, 1973.

Lewis, David. *On the Plurality of Worlds*. Oxford: Wiley-Blackwell, 1986.

Linsky, Bernard, and Edward N. Zalta. "In Defense of the Simplest Quantified Modal Logic." *Philosophical Perspectives* 8 (1994): 431–58.

Linsky, Bernard, and Edward N. Zalta. "In Defense of the Contingently Nonconcrete." *Philosophical Studies* 84, nos. 2–3 (1996): 283–94.

Lycan, William G. "The Trouble with Possible Worlds." In *The Possible and the Actual*, edited by Michael J. Loux. Ithaca: Cornell University Press, 1979.

Lycan, William G. *Modality and Meaning*. Dordrecht: Kluwer, 1994.

Malebranche, N. *Philosophical Selections*. Edited by Steven Nadler. Indianapolis: Hackett, 1992.

Mann, William E. "Divine Simplicity." *Religious Studies* 18, no. 4 (1982): 451–71.

Mares, Edwin D. "Who's Afraid of Impossible Worlds?" *Notre Dame Journal of Formal Logic* 38, no. 4 (1997): 516–26.

Mates, Benson. *The Philosophy of Leibniz: Metaphysics and Language*. New York: Oxford University Press, 1986.

McGinn, Colin. *Logical Properties: Identity, Existence, Predication, Necessity, Truth*. Oxford: Oxford University Press, 2000.

McGinn, Colin. *Consciousness and Its Objects*. Oxford: Oxford University Press, 2004.

McMichael, Alan. "A Problem for Actualism about Possible Worlds." *The Philosophical Review* 92, no. 1 (1983): 49–66.

Meinong, Alexius. "On the Theory of Objects." In *Realism and the Background of Phenomenology*, edited by Roderick M. Chisholm, 76–117. Glencoe: Free Press, 1960.

Menzel, Christopher. "Actualism, Ontological Commitment, and Possible World Semantics." *Synthese* 85, no. 3 (1990): 355–89.

Menzel, Christopher. "The True Modal Logic." *Journal of Philosophical Logic* 20, no. 4 (1991): 331–74.

Menzel, Christopher. "Possibilism and Object Theory." *Philosophical Studies* 69, no. 2/3 (1993a): 195–208.

Menzel, Christopher. "Singular Propositions and Modal Logic." *Philosophical Topics* 21, no. 2 (Philosophy of Logic) (1993b): 113–48.

Menzel, Christopher. "In Defense of the Possibilism–Actualism Distinction." *Philosophical Studies* 177, no. 7 (2020): 1971–97.

Merricks, Trenton. *Truth and Ontology*. Oxford: Oxford University Press, 2007.

Merricks, Trenton. *Propositions*. Oxford: Oxford University Press, 2015.

Miller, Barry. *The Fullness of Being: A New Paradigm for Existence*. Notre Dame: University of Notre Dame Press, 2012.

Moore, G. E. "Is Existence a Predicate?" In *Philosophical Papers*, 114–26. New York: Collier, 1959.

Morris, Thomas, and Christopher Menzel. "Absolute Creation." *American Philosophical Quarterly* 23, no. 4 (1986): 353–62.

Morris, Thomas. "Perfect Being Theology." *Noûs* 21, no. 1 (1987): 19–30.

Morris, Thomas. *Anselmian Explorations: Essays in Philosophical Theology*. Notre Dame: University of Notre Dame Press, 1989.

Mourant, John A. *Introduction to the Ideas of St. Augustine*. Pennsylvania: Penn State University Park, 1964.

Murday, Brendan. "Names and Obstinate Rigidity." *Southern Journal of Philosophy* 51, no. 2 (2013): 224–42.

Nagasawa, Yujin. *Maximal God: A New Defence of Perfect Being Theism*. Oxford: Oxford University Press, 2017.

Nelson, Michael, and Edward Zalta. "Bennett and 'Proxy Actualism.'" *Philosophical Studies* 142, no. 2 (2009): 277–92.

Nolan, Daniel. "Impossible Worlds: A Modest Approach." *Notre Dame Journal of Formal Logic* 38, no. 4 (1997): 535–72.

Parsons, Terrence. *Nonexistent Objects*. New Haven: Yale University Press, 1980.

Paśniczek, Jacek. "Can Meinongian Logic Be Free?" In *New Essays in Free Logic*, edited by Edgar Morscher and Alexander Hieke, 227–39. Dordrecht: Springer, 2001.

Perszyk, Ken. *Molinism: The Contemporary Debate*. Oxford: Oxford University Press, 2011.

Plantinga, Alvin. "Kant's Objection to the Ontological Argument." *Journal of Philosophy* 63, no. 19 (1966): 537–46.

Plantinga, Alvin. *The Nature of Necessity*. Oxford: Oxford University Press, 1974.

Plantinga, Alvin. "The Boethian Compromise." *American Philosophical Quarterly* 15, no. 2 (1978): 129–38. In Plantinga 2003b.

Plantinga, Alvin. "De Essentia." *Grazer Philosophische Studien* 7, no. 1 (1979): 101–21. Page references to Plantinga 2003b.

Plantinga, Alvin. *Does God Have a Nature?* Milwaukee: Marquette University Press, 1980.

Plantinga, Alvin. "How to Be an Anti-realist." *Proceedings and Addresses of the American Philosophical Association* 56, no. 1 (1982): 47–70.

Plantinga, Alvin. "On Existentialism." *Philosophical Studies* 44, no. 1 (1983): 1–20. In Plantinga 2003b.

Plantinga, Alvin. "Replies to My Colleagues." In *Alvin Plantinga*, edited by James Tomberlin and Peter van Inwagen, 313–96. Dordrecht: Springer Netherlands, 1985a.

Plantinga, Alvin. "Self-Profile." In *Alvin Plantinga*, edited by James Tomberlin and Peter van Inwagen, 3–97. Dordrecht: Springer Netherlands, 1985b.

Plantinga, Alvin. "Two Concepts of Modality: Modal Realism and Modal Reductionism." *Philosophical Perspectives* 1 (1987): 189–231. In Plantinga 2003b.

Plantinga, Alvin. "Actualism and Possible Worlds." In *Essays in the Metaphysics of Modality*, edited by Matthew Davidson, 103–22. New York: Oxford, 2003a.

Plantinga, Alvin. *Essays in the Metaphysics of Modality*. Edited by Matthew Davidson. New York: Oxford University Press, 2003b.

Pollock, John L. *The Foundations of Philosophical Semantics*. Princeton: Princeton University Press, 1984.

Pollock, John L. "Plantinga on Possible Worlds." In *Alvin Plantinga*, edited by James Tomberlin and Peter van Inwagen, 121–44. Dordrecht: Springer Netherlands, 1985.

Priest, Graham. *Towards Non-being: The Logic and Metaphysics of Intentionality*. 1st ed. Oxford: Oxford University Press, 2005.

Priest, Graham. "Replies to Nolan and Kroon." *Philosophy and Phenomenological Research* 76, no. 1 (2008): 208–14.

Priest, Graham. *Towards Non-being: The Logic and Metaphysics of Intentionality*. 2nd ed. Oxford: Oxford University Press, 2016.
Prior, A. N. *Time and Modality*. Westport: Greenwood Press, 1957.
Prior, A. N. "Identifiable Individuals." In *Papers on Time and Tense*, 66–78. Oxford: Oxford University Press, 1968.
Prior, A. N. "The Possibly-True and the Possible." In *Papers in Logic and Ethics*, 202–14. Amherst: Massachusetts, 1976.
Prior, A. N., and Kit Fine. *Worlds, Times, and Selves*. Amherst: Massachusetts, 1977.
Quine, W. V. "On What There Is." In *From a Logical Point of View*, edited by W. V. Quine. Cambridge: Harvard University Press, 1953.
Quine, W. V. *Word & Object*. Cambridge: MIT Press, 1960.
The Qur'an. Translated by M. A. S. Abdel Haleem. Oxford: Oxford University Press, 2004.
Rapaport, William J. "Meinongian Theories and a Russellian Paradox." *Noûs* 12, no. 2 (1978): 153–80.
Reimer, Marga. "The Problem of Empty Names." *Australasian Journal of Philosophy* 79, no. 4 (2001): 491–506.
Rhoda, Alan R. "Presentism, Truthmakers, and God." *Pacific Philosophical Quarterly* 90, no. 1 (2009): 41–62.
Rodriguez-Pereyra, Gonzalo. "Why Truthmakers?" In *Truthmakers: The Contemporary Debate*, edited by Helen Beebee and Julian Dodd, 17–32. Oxford: Oxford University Press, 2005.
Rosen, Gideon. "Metaphysical Dependence: Grounding and Reduction." In *Modality: Metaphysics, Logic, and Epistemology*, edited by Bob Hale and Aviv Hoffmann, 109–37. Oxford: Oxford University Press, 2010.
Rosenkrantz, Gary S. *Haecceity: An Ontological Essay*. Dordrecht: Springer, 1993.
Routley, Richard. *Exploring Meinong's Jungle and Beyond*. Edited by Maureen Eckert. Dordrecht: Springer, 2018. (Originally 1980.)
Roy, Tony, and Matthew Davidson. "New Directions in Metaphysics." In *The Continuum Companion to Metaphysics*, edited by Neil A. Manson and Robert W. Barnard, 268–91. London: Continuum, 2012.
Russell, Bertrand. *The Principles of Mathematics*. London: George Allen and Unwin, 1903.
Russell, Bertrand. "On Denoting." *Mind* 14, no. 56 (1905): 479–93.
Russell, Bertrand. "On the Nature of Truth and Falsehood." In *Philosophical Essays*, 147–59. Oxford: Routledge, 1910.
Russell, Bertrand. "Knowledge by Acquaintance and Knowledge by Description." In *Mysticism and Logic*, 209–32. New York: Doubleday, 1917.

Russell, Bertrand. "Review of A. Meinong Untersuchungen zur Gegenstandstheorie und Psychologie." In *Essays on Analysis*, edited by Douglas Lackey. New York: George Braziller, 1973.

Russell, Bertrand. "The Philosophy of Logical Atomism." In *Logic and Knowledge*, edited by Robert C. Marsh, 175–283. Sydney: Allen & Unwin, 1956.

Ryle, Gilbert. "Systematically Misleading Expressions." In *Logic and Language, First Series*, edited by Anthony Flew, 11–37. Oxford: Blackwell, 1960.

Salmon, Nathan. *Reference and Essence*. Princeton: Princeton University Press, 1981.

Salmon, Nathan. *Frege's Puzzle*. Atascadero: Ridgeview, 1986.

Salmon, Nathan. "Existence." *Philosophical Perspectives* 1 (1987): 49–108.

Salmon, Nathan. "Nonexistence." *Noûs* 32, no. 3 (1998): 277–319.

Schaffer, Jonathan. "On What Grounds What." In *Metametaphysics: New Essays on the Foundations of Ontology*, edited by David Manley, David J. Chalmers, and Ryan Wasserman, 347–84. Oxford: Oxford University Press, 2009.

Schiffer, Stephen. *The Things We Mean*. Oxford: Oxford University Press, 2003.

Sider, Theodore. *Four-Dimensionalism: An Ontology of Persistence and Time*. Oxford: Oxford University Press, 2001.

Soames, Scott. *Beyond Rigidity: The Unfinished Semantic Agenda of Naming and Necessity*. Oxford: Oxford University Press, 2002.

Speaks, Jeff. "On Possibly Nonexistent Propositions." *Philosophy and Phenomenological Research* 85, no. 3 (2012): 528–62.

Stalnaker, Robert. "Merely Possible Propositions." In *Modality: Metaphysics, Logic, and Epistemology*, edited by Bob Hale and Aviv Hoffman, 21–33. Oxford: Oxford University Press, 2010.

Stalnaker, Robert. *Mere Possibilities: Metaphysical Foundations of Modal Semantics*. Princeton: Princeton University Press, 2012.

Stebbing, L. S. *A Modern Introduction to Logic*. London: Methuen, 1950.

Stephanou, Yannis. "Serious Actualism." *The Philosophical Review* 116, no. 2 (2007): 219–50.

Stump, Eleonore, and Norman Kretzmann. "Absolute Simplicity." *Faith and Philosophy* 2, no. 4 (1985): 353–82.

Stump, Eleonore. "Simplicity." In *A Companion to the Philosophy of Religion*, edited by Charles Taliaferro, Paul Draper, and Philip L. Quinn, 270–7. Oxford: Wiley Blackwell, 2010.

Taylor, Ken C. "Emptiness without Compromise: A Referentialist Semantics for Empty Names." In *Empty Names, Fiction, and the Puzzles of Nonexistence*, edited by Thomas Hofweber and Anthony Everett, 17–37. Stanford: CSLI, 2000.

Thomasson, Amie L. *Fiction and Metaphysics*. Cambridge: Cambridge University Press, 1998.
Tomberlin, James E., and Frank McGuinness. "Troubles with Actualism." *Philosophical Perspectives* 8 (1994): 459–66.
Tomberlin, James E. "Actualism or Possibilism." *Philosophical Studies* 84 (1996): 263–81.
Turner, Jason. "Strong and Weak Possibility." *Philosophical Studies* 125, no. 2 (2005): 191–217.
Vallicella, William F. *A Paradigm Theory of Existence: Onto-Theology Vindicated*. Dordrecht: Springer, 2002.
Van Cleve, James. *Problems from Kant*. New York: Oxford University Press, 1999.
Van Cleve, James. *Problems from Reid*. Oxford: Oxford University Press, 2015.
Van Cleve, James. "There Are No Necessary Connections between Distinct Existences." Forthcoming.
Van Inwagen, Peter. "Creatures of Fiction." *American Philosophical Quarterly* 14, no. 4 (1977): 299–308.
Van Inwagen, Peter. "Two Concepts of Possible Worlds." *Midwest Studies in Philosophy* 11 (1986): 185–213.
Van Inwagen, Peter. "God and Other Uncreated Things." In *Metaphysics and God: Essays in Honor of Eleonore Stump*, edited by Kevin Timpe, 3–21. Oxford: Routledge, 2009.
Van Inwagen, Peter. "'Who Sees Not That All the Dispute Is about a Word?' Some Thoughts on Bennett's "Proxy 'Actualism.'" *Hungarian Philosophical Review* 3 (2012): 69–81.
Van Inwagen, Peter. "Being, Existence, and Ontological Commitment." In *Existence: Essays in Ontology*, 50–87. Cambridge: Cambridge University Press, 2014a.
Van Inwagen, Peter. *Existence: Essays in Ontology*. Cambridge: Cambridge University Press, 2014b.
Van Inwagen, Peter. "Existence, Ontological Commitment, and Fictional Entities." In *Existence: Essays in Ontology*, 87–116. Cambridge: Cambridge University Press, 2014c.
Vander Laan, David. "Counterpossibles and Similarity." In *Lewisian Themes: The Philosophy of David K. Lewis*, edited by Frank Jackson and Graham Priest, 258–77. Oxford: Clarendon Press, 2004.
Welty, Greg. "Theistic Conceptual Realism." In *Beyond the Control of God? Six Views on the Problem of God and Abstract Objects*, edited by Paul M. Gould, 81–96. New York: Bloomsbury, 2014.

Wierenga, Edward. "Theism and Counterpossibles." *Philosophical Studies* 89, no. 1 (1998): 87–103.
Williams, C. J. F. *What Is Existence?* Oxford: Clarendon Press, 1981.
Williams, Donald. "Mind as a Matter of Fact." *The Review of Metaphysics* 13, no. 2 (1959): 203–25.
Williamson, Timothy. "Necessary Existents." In *Royal Institute of Philosophy Supplement*, edited by Anthony O'Hear, vol. 51, 233–51. Cambridge: Cambridge University Press, 2002.
Williamson, Timothy. *Modal Logic as Metaphysics*. Oxford: Oxford University Press, 2013.
Wolterstorff, Nicholas. *On Universals*. Chicago: University of Chicago Press, 1970.
Wolterstorff, Nicholas. "Divine Simplicity." *Philosophical Perspectives* 5 (1991): 531–52.
Yagisawa, Takashi. "A New Argument against the Existence Requirement." *Analysis* 65, no. 1 (2005): 39–42.
Zalta, Edward. *Abstract Objects: An Introduction to Axiomatic Metaphysics*. Dordrecht: Kluwer, 1983.
Zalta, Edward N. *Intensional Logic and the Metaphysics of Intentionality*. Cambridge: MIT Press, 1988.
Zemach, E. M. "Existence and Nonexistents." *Erkenntnis* 39, no. 2 (1993): 145–66.
Zwicky, Arnold, and Jerrold Sadock. "Ambiguity Tests and How to Fail Them." In *Syntax and Semantics*, edited by John P. Kimball, vol. 4, 1–36. Leiden: Brill, 1975.

Index

abstract objects 42–3, 60, 64, 97, 104, 114, 119–23, 135, 139–58
actualism 1–11, 20–2, 59–65, 94–5
  frivolous 11
  serious 1, 11, 13–27, 29–32, 92, 95, 101, 103, 105, 109
Adams, Robert 5–7, 51–2, 91–8, 102
ambiguity 102–3, 123–5
Aquinas, Thomas 151
asiety, divine 143–5, 158
Augustine 151
Avicenna 151
Ayer, A. J. 80

Bencivenga, Ermanno 9
Bennett, Karen 6
Bergmann, Michael 6, 20–5, 27
Bergmann, Michael and Brower, Jeffrey 147, 152
Berkeley, George 77
Berto, Francisco 121
Berto, Francisco and Priest, Graham 128–9
Braun, David 48, 63
Bueno, Otavio and Zalta, Edward 118–19

Cameron, Ross 33
Carnap, Rudolph 79
Chisholm, Roderick 60, 135
Cocchiarella, Nino B. 10
Craig, William Lane 154–5
Crane, Tim 34–5, 124–5, 132, 134, 136
Crisp, Thomas 6, 42

Descartes, René 71, 77, 143–5
direct reference 46–50, 63, 87, 90, 92, 94, 107
Divine Foreknowledge 54–5
Donnellan, Keith 48, 63

empty terms 46–52, 87–90
eternalism 43, 45

Everett, Anthony 129
existentialism 1, 17, 46, 91–111

fictional characters 63–6, 81, 115, 119, 121, 124, 126, 129–31, 136–7
Fine, Kit ix, 102, 108–11, 140
Fitch, G. W. 7, 93
Forrest, Peter 33
Frege, Gottlob 78

Gould, Paul M. and Davis, Richard B. 155–6
grounding, metaphysical 139–41
growing block theory of time 32–3

haecceities 1, 56, 57, 69, 87, 91, 94–8, 100, 149
Hinchliff, Mark 9, 132
Hudson, Hud 20, 23
Hume, David 77
Hume's Dictum 99

independence thesis 1, 3, 13–14, 29, 36, 55–6, 59

Jacquette, Dale 38, 60, 64, 114–15, 117–19, 121

Kant, Immanuel 77, 78
Kripke, Saul 30–1, 56, 63, 87–8, 95–6, 100, 130
Kripke semantics 96, 100
Kroon, Frederick 126–7

Lambert, Karel ix, 10
Leibniz, G. W. 13, 145–6
Lewis, David 7, 8, 36, 37, 38, 122, 150
Linsky Bernard, and Zalta Edward 7, 33, 49, 101
Lucretianism 42, 43
Lycan, William 3

Malebanche, Nicholas 13
McGinn, Colin 35, 83–6
McMichael, Alan 95–6
Meinong, Alexius 3, 8, 59, 114–15
Meinongianism 1–5, 9–11, 24, 51, 59–66, 95–6, 98, 112–13
Meinongianism, Deflationary 113–37
Meinongianism, modal 125–8
Meinongianism, Robust 113–37
Menzel, Christopher 6, 57, 96, 98
Merricks, Trenton 42–3
Miller, Barry 71
Molinism 52–4
Moore, G. E. 82
Morris, Thomas and Menzel, Christopher 145–9
Moving Spotlight Theory 33

negative existentials 51, 73–5, 81, 87–90, 136
Nelson, Michael and Zalta, Edward 6
Newton, Isaac 157–8
nonexistent objects 6, 81, 93, 95–6, 98, 113–15, 117–20, 122, 124–5, 127–37

Parsons, Terrence 4, 7, 10, 34, 38, 65, 115–18, 120, 131
Paśniczek, Jacek 10
perfect being theology 142–3, 153–4
Plantinga, Alvin ix, 1, 2, 6–7, 11, 14–20, 30–1, 49, 56, 91, 95, 96, 98–110, 150–2
Pollock, John ix, 31
presentism 1, 27, 28, 29, 41, 42, 43
 cross-time relations 44–6
 grounding problems 41–4
 serious 13–14, 27–9
Priest, Graham 34, 125–8, 132–3, 136–7
Prior, Arthur 28–9, 108–9
properties
 pleonastic 35, 124
 world-indexed 30, 69, 87
propositions 2, 37, 41, 43, 45–53, 67, 69, 81, 83–4, 88–91, 150–1
 singular 1, 17, 32, 46–50, 91–4, 100–8

Quine, W. V. 7, 62, 68, 73

Rapaport, William J. 119
rigid designation 31, 46, 48–9, 51, 55–6, 63, 67, 85–9, 107
Routley, Richard 7, 34, 38, 63–4, 115–17, 120, 131
Russell, Bertrand 4, 7–8, 72, 79, 82, 114
Ryle, Gilbert 80

Salmon, Nathan ix, 3, 31–4, 46, 48, 55, 64, 70–1, 136
Sib 46–52, 98, 105–6
Speaks, Jeff 105–6
Spinoza, Baruch 151
Stalnaker, Robert 103–4
Stebbing, L. S. 79–80
Stephanou, Yannis 25, 26

theistic activism 146–9, 155–6
theistic emanationism 145–9, 155–6
theistic mentalism 149–52
theistic platonism 152–4
theistic voluntarism 143–5
Thomasson, Amie 64, 136
Tomberlin, James and McGuinness, Frank 135–6
Transworld Property Exemplification 21–5
truth, inside and outside 102–6
Turner, Jason 104–5

Vallicella, William 71, 75, 76
Van Cleve, James 78
Van Inwagen, Peter 4–5, 8, 64, 70, 81, 136, 142–3, 152–4, 158

Welty, Greg 149
Williamson, Timothy 33, 92–4, 101

Yagisawa, Takashi 29–31

Zalta, Edward 10, 118–24, 135–7

www.ingramcontent.com/pod-product-compliance
Lightning Source LLC
Chambersburg PA
CBHW061835300426
44115CB00013B/2396